D1636757

# RAHAB
## AND OTHER
# MIRACLES

JIMMY SWAGGART

# RAHAB
## AND OTHER
# MIRACLES

JIMMY SWAGGART MINISTRIES
P.O. Box 262550 | Baton Rouge, Louisiana 70826-2550
www.jsm.org

ISBN 978-1-941403-71-6

09-174 | COPYRIGHT © 2021 Jimmy Swaggart Ministries®

21 22 23 24 25 26 27 28 29 30 / Sheridan / 10 9 8 7 6 5 4 3 2 1

# TABLE OF CONTENTS

INTRODUCTION . . . . . . . . . . . . . . . . . . . . . . . . . . . . . . . . . . . . . . . 1

CHAPTER 1    The Lord Spoke to Joshua . . . . . . . . . . . . . . . . . . 9

CHAPTER 2    The Precious Blood of Christ . . . . . . . . . . . . . . 41

CHAPTER 3    Tomorrow the Lord Will Do

Wonders among You. . . . . . . . . . . . . . . . . . . . . . 71

CHAPTER 4    The Miracle . . . . . . . . . . . . . . . . . . . . . . . . . . . 101

CHAPTER 5    God's Plan for the Fall of Jericho . . . . . . . . . 133

CHAPTER 6    Trespass . . . . . . . . . . . . . . . . . . . . . . . . . . . . . . 163

CHAPTER 7    Valley of Achor . . . . . . . . . . . . . . . . . . . . . . . . 195

REFERENCES . . . . . . . . . . . . . . . . . . . . . . . . . . . . . . . . . . . . . . 217

# RAHAB
## AND OTHER
# MIRACLES

INTRODUCTION

# INTRODUCTION

WE HAVE NO INFORMATION at all as it regards the birth of Joshua, except we know by the matter of deduction that he was born in Egypt. As well, by the same method, we know that he was more than twenty years of age when Moses led the children of Israel out of bondage. And yet, he was one of the greatest men of God who ever lived.

The Hebrew name *Joshua* is *Jesus* in the Greek. So the Joshua who led the children of Israel into the promised land was a prefigurement of the Christ of glory who leads the child of God into the spiritual promised land.

Many have thought that the land of promise was a type of heaven; it is not. It is a physical type of the spiritual inheritance given to us in this great Christian walk. There were Jebusites, Hivites, Canaanites, and others in the land of promise. These were enemies of God's people. There is not such in heaven.

## THE DIVINE GREETING

*"Moses My servant is dead."* Such is the divine greeting to the already aged Joshua with which the book that bears his name opens. He was more than sixty years of age by now. It was a message that must have tried even his fortitude; who could

follow Moses? In addition, the message came from Him who alone could send it with assurance of perfect certitude. Moses was dead, and it was just at the very moment, it would seem, when his people and those who had helped him to lead them needed his guidance most. However, God's ways are not our ways. Moses was dead, but God was not dead!

Joshua had been anointed by Moses before the assent of the lawgiver to Mount Pisgah, from which he would not return. In fact, the people of Israel were never to see him again or even to know where his remains were laid. They must now be content with the guidance of Moses' minister (Ex. 24:13; Num. 27:18; Deut. 1:38). It would seem that they loyally accepted Joshua. Certainly he accepted, with childlike trust and simplicity, the high but heavy charge that was thus suddenly laid on him. Neither elated nor pressed by it, he at once set to work to carry out the divine command. In fact, the entirety of his remaining years was a calm, unwavering response to the exhortation of Jehovah.

## VICTORIES

As it regards his great work, one might say that the victories of Joshua that we will study were not only the subject of prophecy, one might say, but they were a prophecy themselves. They were a type and earnest of the blessings that Jehovah had in store for His people. On their darker side, they were a type and an earnest of His judgments upon those who refused to know Him and, tragically, found themselves fighting against Him.

So we see in the life of Joshua that the victories of the spiritual and military leader are a microcosm of ourselves, and that it is meant to be! As Joshua took the land, we are, as well, to occupy that which the Lord has given us. We are also to hold it until we die or the trump beckons us home. There are many enemies there, and within the natural, they cannot be conquered. However, if we follow the Lord as Joshua followed the Lord, and, in effect, showed us the way, we will find these victories in our experience as he found them in his. God has the way, and we must not veer from that way.

## JOSHUA AS A TYPE OF CHRIST

I think that as we go through the experiences of Joshua, it will be easy to see the conqueror as a type of Christ:

- Joshua began his life by sharing the sufferings of his brethren in Egypt; so Jesus took upon Him the form of a servant and shared the lot of His brethren.
- The imperfect work of Moses was taken up and completed by Joshua to a far lesser degree than that which was taken up and completed by Christ. In other words, the law was perfected in the gospel.
- In accordance with their common name, both Joshua and Jesus saved the people given to them from their enemies.
- Both *"went forth conquering and to conquer,"* and both conquered after being at first apparently defeated through the sins of others.

- Joshua brought the chosen people into the promised land and gave them rest and a home in it. Jesus brings the elect into the kingdom prepared for us and gives us rest and an eternal home in the many mansions of the Father.

- Both Joshua and our Lord entered into their ministry on the banks of the Jordan River. Jesus, as the captain, appeared to Joshua on those banks, while God spoke concerning Christ on the banks of that Jordan.

- The Passover kept by Joshua and the children of Israel on the banks of Jordan proclaimed the crucifixion of Christ, who paid the supreme price in order to rescue the fallen sons of Adam's lost race.

- Under Joshua, the passage of Jordan as the road to the land of promise was freed from difficulty and danger. The river of death by which we must enter into our rest has been robbed of its terrors by Christ. Because He lives, we shall live also.

- The twelve stones taken from the bed of the Jordan River and set up as witnesses to the people of their deliverance may represent the twelve apostles who were living witnesses of His resurrection, which guaranteed our resurrection as well.

- When he had completed his work, Joshua ascended the mountain of Ephraim and dwelt in security from his enemies. Having finished the work that the Father gave him to do (John 17:4), Jesus ascended up on high and *"sat down on the right hand of God; From henceforth expecting till his enemies be made His footstool"* (Heb. 10:12-13).

Trust Him when thy wants are many;
Trust Him when thy friends are few;
And the time of swift temptation
Is the time to trust Him too.

Trust Him when thy soul is burdened
With the sense of all its sin;
He will speak the word of pardon,
He will make thee clean within.

Trust Him for the grace sufficient,
Ever equal to thy need;
Trust Him always for the answer,
When in His dear name you plead.

Trust Him for the grace to conquer,
He is able to subdue;
Trust Him for the power for service;
Trust Him for the blessing too.

Trust Him when dark doubts assail thee,
Trust Him when thy strength is small.
Trust Him when to simply trust Him
Seems the hardest thing of all.

Trust Him, He is ever faithful;
Trust Him, for His will is best;
Trust Him; for the heart of Jesus
Is the only place of rest.

# RAHAB

## AND OTHER

# MIRACLES

## THE LORD SPOKE
## TO JOSHUA

# THE LORD SPOKE TO JOSHUA

*"NOW AFTER THE DEATH of Moses the servant of the Lord it came to pass, that the Lord spake unto Joshua the son of Nun, Moses' minister, saying, Moses my servant is dead; now therefore arise, go over this Jordan, thou, and all this people, unto the land which I do give to them, even to the children of Israel. Every place that the sole of your foot shall tread upon, that have I given unto you, as I said unto Moses. From the wilderness and this Lebanon even unto the great river, the river Euphrates, all the land of the Hittites, and unto the great sea toward the going down of the sun, shall be your coast. There shall not any man be able to stand before thee all the days of thy life: as I was with Moses, so I will be with thee: I will not fail thee, nor forsake thee"* (Josh. 1:1-5).

## NOW AFTER THE DEATH OF MOSES
## THE SERVANT OF THE LORD

We are beginning with the story of Joshua at the juncture of the passing of Moses when, in reality, the great warrior made his debut nearly forty years earlier when he fought with Amalek (Ex. 17:8-16). Then we have Joshua and Caleb who went with others into the land of Israel to reconnoiter what was there. Joshua and Caleb came back with a glowing report of faith, but, unfortunately, the other men with them did not see it that way. Their unbelief doomed the entire generation of Israel to die in the wilderness, with the exception of Joshua and Caleb (Num. 14:36-39).

Now Moses was dead, and the Holy Spirit placed on the shoulders of Joshua the charge as it regarded the taking of the land that would later be called Israel. To be sure, it was a monumental task. But yet, if those whom the Lord called would only evidence faith, without fail, He would give them the strength and ability, plus the wisdom and the knowledge, to get the job done. The Lord never calls someone for a task but that He equips that person for that task, as He did Joshua.

## THE PLAN OF GOD

When we read Joshua 1, we see that God had planned that which Israel was to do. He said to Joshua, *"Go over this Jordan, thou, and all this people, unto the land which I do give to them, even to the children of Israel."* But yet, despite the fact that the Lord had given them the land, it was still possessed by the Hittites, plus other tribes, with the Hittites being some of the fiercest men in that part of the world at that particular time.

Actually, I saw part of a documentary that was shown over television, which denoted the fierceness and power of the Hittites.

In the natural, Israel would be no match for this tribe, plus the many others in that part of the world, but they were not to do things in the natural. They were to have the help of God, and in that case, the Hittites, plus others, didn't have a chance, even as we shall see later as it regards the great victories given to Joshua.

As God had a plan for Israel, even with the boundaries drawn off, likewise, He has a plan for every single believer on the face of the earth. God never saves someone for him to just languish until he dies. He saves us for many reasons, and to be sure, He has a plan for each and every believer. If the believer will ardently seek the face of the Lord, to be sure, the Lord will outline that plan for such a person.

However, if it's something we devise ourselves, we will not have the help of the Lord. Unfortunately, all too often that is what takes place in Christian circles. People do not know what God really wants them to do, and they set on a course designed by themselves, which is guaranteed of failure. If the believer will seek the Lord and ask for leading and direction, to be sure, the Lord will answer such a prayer.

## DAVID

The great songwriter said, *"The LORD is the portion of mine inheritance and of my cup: Thou maintainest my lot. The lines are fallen unto me in pleasant places; yea, I have a goodly heritage"* (Ps. 16:5-6).

David here plainly says that the Lord had drawn the boundaries of David's life and ministry, which He desires to do for all. We must here remember that those lines were drawn in pleasant places.

There are many Christians who have an erroneous idea of the will of God. They are afraid to seek the Lord as it regards what He wants them to do, fearing that He will want something that they have no desire to do whatsoever. Nothing could be more wrong.

Whatever it is that God wants a person to do and, thereby, calls that person to perform that task, to be sure, the Lord will without fail put a love in that person's heart for that thing and that place, wherever and whatever it might be. It will make that person miserable if he is any place other than these *"pleasant places."* Again, allow us to state the fact that it will always be pleasant if the Lord is doing the doing.

Certainly, what the Lord had designed for Joshua was momentous indeed. In fact, there was no way that Joshua could carry out this task unless the Lord would be with him. To be sure, the Lord had promised to be with him. He said, *"As I was with Moses, so I will be with thee: I will not fail thee, nor forsake thee"* (Josh. 1:5).

Now the Lord would give Joshua tremendous promises, so tremendous that they defy description. As we read these promises, we should understand that the Lord is saying the same thing to us that He said to Joshua. Read it, take it, and believe it because, *"thus saith the Lord"*:

> *Be strong and of a good courage: for unto this people shalt thou*
> *divide for an inheritance the land, which I sware unto their*

*fathers to give them. Only be thou strong and very courageous, that thou mayest observe to do according to all the law, which Moses my servant commanded thee: turn not from it to the right hand or to the left, that thou mayest prosper whithersoever thou goest. This book of the law shall not depart out of thy mouth; but thou shalt meditate therein day and night, that thou mayest observe to do according to all that is written therein: for then thou shalt make thy way prosperous, and then thou shalt have good success. Have not I commanded thee? Be strong and of a good courage; be not afraid, neither be thou dismayed: for the* Lord *thy God is with thee withersoever thou goest* (Josh. 1:6-9).

## BE STRONG

Three times in these four verses the Lord told Joshua (and you and me) to be strong. Why would He say that?

It was because Satan would come against Joshua in every capacity possible by using these powerful tribes. Likewise, Satan will do the very same thing to you and me. Therefore, we have to be strong and stand up to him, and never forget the promises of God.

Joshua began his ministry on the banks of Jordan, where Christ was baptized, and entered upon the public exercise of his prophetic office. I'm sure the reader knows that the name Joshua is the Hebrew derivative of the Greek *Jesus,* the name of our blessed Lord Himself. Israel had dwelt in the wilderness for some forty years, but it was now time for them to go into the promised land.

It was not God's will that one foot breadth was to rest in the hands of its former owners; likewise, it is presently the intent of the Holy Spirit for everything in our lives to be removed that hinders our progress with the Lord. It is God's will that we possess the entirety of the promise, which pertains to total victory over the world, the flesh, and the devil (James 4:5).

Incidentally, the area of Joshua 1:4 includes modern Syria, Jordan, part of Iraq, and the Arab Peninsula. All of this was never actually in the hands of the Israelites, except during the reigns of David and Solomon; however, during the coming kingdom age, Israel will possess all of that and more.

## POSSESSING THE LAND

Bible scholar George Williams said:

Moses, as representing the law, could not bring Israel into the promised land; he must die, for he had made one failure under that law, and possession of Canaan by law could only be by a perfect obedience to it, which man could not render. Man, being a sinner, cannot give this perfect obedience. Joshua, a type of the risen Saviour, brought Israel into the goodly land. Grace, operating in the power of the Holy Spirit, which it always does, can bring men into the employment of that which the law, because of man's moral weakness on which it acts, can never do.[1]

Joshua's success depended upon his obedience to two factors:

1.  The eternal Word, who is the Lord of Hosts.
2.  The written Word manifested in Joshua 1:8.

Obedience to these two gives a victorious Christian experience. We find in this that prosperity depended upon a strict adherence to the law of God. Whereas Israel at that time only had a partial revelation—the law—, we now have the entirety of the revelation of God, given in the entirety of His Word. It, and it alone, portrays the way. To deviate from the Word of God is to deviate from prosperity. To adhere to the Word of God is to prosper, and to prosper in all things.

## THE COMMISSION

The Lord had promised this great land to the children of Israel; however, promise is one thing, but possession is another. God said, "I, even I, do give you the land." Such was the promise, but the one condition of possession was the placing of the foot upon it. This meant war, and to be certain, Satan will contest our advance every foot of the way.

The children of Israel were delivered out of Egypt without any fight or war. God did it all! Likewise, redemption to the new-found Christian is all of God and none of him, with the exception of simply believing. All Israel had to do to be released from Egypt was to believe God. All the sinner has to do to be delivered from satanic bondage is to believe God; however, when it comes to possession of all that God has promised us, that is another matter entirely. We have to fight for every foot of spiritual ground that we take, and Satan does not give ground easily.

## WARFARE

It is warfare, of that there is no debate. Paul told Timothy:

*This charge I commit unto you, son Timothy* (refers to a command or injunction), *according to the prophecies which went before on you* (probably refers to the time frame of Acts 16:1-3), *that you by them might war a good warfare* (we aren't told exactly what the prophecies were, but that they spoke of an assignment to leadership in the army of King Jesus); *Holding faith* (maintaining faith in Christ and the cross), *and a good conscience* (speaks of following the Word of the Lord exactly as it is given); *which some having put away concerning faith have made shipwreck* (a metaphor used by Paul, pointing to those who had abandoned the cross) (I Tim. 1:18-19). – The Expositor's Study Bible

That there will be war, there is no doubt; however, the great contention is how this war is to be conducted. On this rests defeat or victory. Regrettably, most of the modern church has no idea how this warfare is to be conducted, how it is to be addressed, or how it is to be fought. If it is to be noticed, as it regards this warfare, Paul told Timothy that he must hold faith.

What did the apostle mean by that?

He then said in the same epistle:

*Fight the good fight of faith* (in essence, the only fight we're called upon to engage; every attack by Satan against the believer, irrespective of its form, is to destroy or at least to seriously weaken our faith; he wants to push our faith from the cross to other things), *lay hold on eternal life* (we do such by understanding that all life comes from Christ, and the means is the cross), *whereunto you are also called* (called to follow Christ), *and have professed a good profession before many witnesses.* (This does not refer to a particular occasion, but to the entirety of his life for Christ)" (I Tim. 6:12) – The Expositor's Study Bible

This is the only fight that we are called upon to engage— the good fight of faith. In a sense, that is the same thing as holding faith.

Now again, what did Paul mean by that?

## FIGHT THE GOOD FIGHT OF FAITH

This fight is in the realm of faith. So, what are we talking about when we mention faith?

Just to use the term *faith* and let it drop there really says nothing. As someone has well said, "Anything that says too much in the end actually says precious little."

When Paul speaks of faith, without exception, he is always speaking of faith in Christ and what Christ did at the cross (Rom. 6:3-14; 8:1-11; I Cor. 1:17-18, 23; 2:2). That is the same thing as believing the Word of God inasmuch as the Word is the story of Christ and Him crucified.

Satan will do everything within his power to stop the believer from placing his faith exclusively in Christ and the cross. To be frank, he doesn't mind too much if your faith is merely in Christ. He knows that if Christ is divorced from the cross, then the means by which God gives us all things has just been removed. Let us say it this way: Christ is the source, and the cross is the means.

## THE CROSS

This refers to the fact that everything that we receive from our Savior, and I mean everything, comes to us by the means of the cross. In other words, we could not have anything from the Lord, be it salvation, the baptism with the Holy Spirit, divine healing, blessings, prosperity, righteousness, fruit and gifts of the Spirit, etc., without the cross. In fact, if one attempts to believe God by placing his or her faith in something other than Christ and the cross, the Jesus that remains is *"another Jesus,"* which means that it is a fabrication (II Cor. 11:4).

To start this book off right and to give us the foundation on which Joshua won all of his victories, which we will see a little later, let us give the following direction:

## GOD'S WAY

- Focus: the Lord Jesus Christ (Col. 2:9-10).
- Object of faith: the cross of Christ (Rom. 6:3-5; Gal. 2:20-21; I Cor. 1:17-18, 23; 2:2).
- Power source: the Holy Spirit (Rom. 8:1-11; Col. 2:10-15; Eph. 2:13-18).
- Results: victory (Rom. 6:14).

Now, the reader should study this diagram very carefully because what you're looking at is God's prescribed order of victory.

Now, let's turn it around and use the same formula but look at it in the manner in which most are presently trying to live for God:

- Focus: works.
- Object of faith: performance.
- Power source: self.
- Results: defeat.

Therefore, the way in which we engage this warfare is by placing our faith exclusively in Christ and what He has done for us at the cross. Then the Holy Spirit, who works exclusively within the legal parameters of the cross of Christ, will grandly and gloriously help us, in fact, guaranteeing victory (Rom. 8:2).

## IS IT A GUARANTEE AGAINST DEFEAT?

In a sense, yes. However, that needs qualification.

While one is most definitely on the right road to victory when one places one's faith exclusively in Christ and the cross, this doesn't mean that Satan is going to fold his tent and leave. In fact, he possibly will gather even greater forces in order to do what he can to stop you. In other words, he is going to test your faith, and test it mightily, and the Lord will give him latitude to do so, up to a point.

In this test of faith, you will fail. It's not, "If I fail," but, "When I fail." There has never been a human being who didn't fail in one way or another; however, there is a difference in the type of failure that results when one is on the right road, than when one is on the wrong road. When one is on the right road, so to speak, even though the failure hurts, still, one knows that there is victory just around the bend. When the Holy Spirit through Paul said, *"Sin shall not have dominion over you"* (Rom. 6:14), He meant exactly what He said. Every believer who has his faith anchored solidly in Christ and the cross can be assured of total and complete victory. To be anchored in Christ and the cross at the same time means that his faith is anchored solidly in the Word. Victory may be some time in coming, and there may be a few battles between now and then, but come it will!

## POSSESSION

As God has designed the promise perfectly, He has also designed possession perfectly. The allowing of great enemies to contest and hinder our progress builds spiritual character, faith, and maturity in the child of God. As we develop the story of Joshua, we are, in effect, studying our own Christian lives. As the blueprint for victory was given by God to Joshua to take the land, likewise, this is the same blueprint for victory in our own lives.

The following has already been given in the overview; however, due to the fact that what has been said is so very, very important, please allow me the latitude of saying it again: Moses, as representing the law, could not bring Israel into the promised land. He must die, for he had made one failure under that law, and possession of Canaan by law could only be by perfect obedience. Man, being a sinner, cannot give this perfect obedience.

Joshua was a type of the risen Savior and would bring Israel into that goodly land. Grace operating in the power of the Holy Spirit can bring men into the enjoyment of that which the law can never fix because of man's moral weakness on which it acts.

## THE RULE OF FAITH

The question is asked, What is the rule of faith? For the Catholic Church, its answer would be, "The church and its teaching." Regrettably, it would be the same for many Protestant churches as well. God's answer is "the Bible."

He said: *"This book of the law shall not depart out of thy mouth; but thou shalt meditate therein day and night, that thou mayest observe to do according to all that is written therein: for then thou shalt make thy way prosperous, and then thou shalt have good success"* (Josh. 1:8). That's about as clear as it can get.

While it is certainly true that the Bible is the rule of faith, and the rule of faith alone, perhaps the following will help us to understand it a little better.

The Bible in its entirety is the story of Jesus Christ and Him crucified (I Cor. 1:23). Actually, the strain of this great truth began immediately after the fall, with the Lord telling Satan through the serpent:

*And I will put enmity* (animosity) *between you and the woman* (presents the Lord now actually speaking to Satan, who had used the serpent; in effect, the Lord is saying to Satan, 'You used the woman to bring down the human race, and I will

use the woman as an instrument to bring the Redeemer into the world who will save the human race'), *and between your seed* (mankind which follows Satan) *and her seed* (the Lord Jesus Christ); *it* (Christ) *shall bruise your head* (the victory that Jesus won at the cross [Col. 2:14-15]), *and you shall bruise His heel* (the sufferings of the cross) (Gen. 3:15).
– The Expositor's Study Bible

It is spelled out plainly in Genesis 4 as it records the saga of Cain and Abel.

## THE FIRST PAGE OF HUMAN HISTORY

We see the sacrificial system instituted on the first page of human history, which was a type of the innocent victim who would come, namely the Lord Jesus Christ, and who would give His life as a sacrifice for dying humanity.

The Lord gave to Abraham the meaning of justification by faith (Gen. 15:6). He even told him how this would be brought about, which would be through the death of an innocent victim. In other words, it was by death that man would be redeemed; however, the Lord did not tell the Patriarch what type of death this would be (Gen. 22:13-14).

It was to Moses that the Lord gave the means by which this death would occur. It would be by the cross (Num. 21:8-9).

Jesus addressed this when He spoke to Nicodemus, saying, *"And as Moses lifted up the serpent in the wilderness, even so must the Son of man be lifted up"* (John 3:14).

He then said: *And I, if I be lifted up from the earth* (refers to His death at Calvary; He was 'lifted up' on the cross; the cross is the foundation of all victory), *will draw all men unto Me* (refers to the salvation of all who come to Him, believing what He did, and trusting in His atoning work). *This He said, signifying what death He should die.* Reynolds says: 'In these words, we learn that the attraction of the cross of Christ will prove to be the mightiest and most sovereign motive ever brought to bear on the human will, and when wielded by the Holy Spirit as a revelation of the matchless love of God, will involve the most sweeping judicial sentence that can be pronounced upon the world and its prince' (John 12:32-33). – The Expositor's Study Bible

## THE WORD OF THE LORD TO JOSHUA

The following verse is very dear to me personally. It says,
*"Have not I commanded thee? Be strong and of a good courage; be not afraid, neither be thou dismayed: for the* LORD *thy God is with thee whithersoever thou goest"* (Josh. 1:9).

Frances and I began in evangelistic work in 1955. Donnie was about two years old. If I remember correctly, the time of which I speak was January 1958. For the previous two years, while preaching meetings here and there, I also held down a full-time job; however, feeling led of the Lord to go full time into evangelistic work, I quit the job I had because I felt that's what the Lord wanted me to do. Our first meeting that January was in a little town in north Louisiana by the name of Sterlington.

I preached two or three nights and then came down so sick that I had to be taken to the hospital. The doctor told me that I had pneumonia.

I transferred to another hospital closer to home. If I remember correctly, I only stayed there one night. The nurse who was on duty, at least when I was there, had about the most profane mouth of any person I've ever seen or heard. Almost every word out of her mouth was profanity.

After staying there the one night, sometime during the next morning, she came into the room and saw me rummaging through the little closet and asked me what I was doing. I related to her, "I'm trying to find my trousers."

She asked, "What are you going to do with your trousers?" only she added a few expletives.

I retorted, "If I can find my pants, I'm going home."

She let me know in no uncertain terms that I was not going to do that, but I persisted. Her parting words were, "If you leave, we are no longer responsible." To be frank, I had no confidence in their responsibility anyway.

Even though I still had pneumonia, Frances drove us home. I was still so sick that I could hardly hold up my head. I was bedridden for the next two or three days, and Satan took full advantage of that.

Almost every time I turned on the radio, I heard a song by one of my cousins. In fact, if I remember correctly, at that time, Jerry Lee (Jerry Lee Lewis) was battling Elvis Presley for the number one spot in the nation. I would turn the dial and one of Mickey's songs would be playing. He ultimately had seventeen number one country and western hits. I would then turn it again, and one of Carl's songs would be airing. All of these were first cousins of mine: Jerry Lee Lewis, Mickey Gilley, and Carl McVoy.

At this time I was so sick I couldn't put my feet on the floor. At the same time, the thoughts went through my mind constantly about how I was going to pay the bills.

## THE TIME OF VICTORY

It was Wednesday night, and Frances and Donnie had gone to Bible study. As I lay there in the bed that night, Satan took full advantage of the situation.

I felt a darkened presence come into that room, and at that time, it was the most powerful I had ever experienced. Satan began to say to me, "How are you going to pay the bills? How are you going to pay the note at the bank for this little house?" Then he said, "You call yourself an evangelist, and you are so sick you cannot even put your feet on the floor. You have no meetings to preach, and the truth is, you'll probably starve to death."

He went on to say, "The man driving Jerry Lee's car makes as much money in a month as you make the entire year. You are a fool."

There isn't a believer who hasn't experienced something of this nature as Satan presses for the kill.

I remember that as I began to pray that night, I was asking the Lord to help me. My Bible was lying by my side on the bed.

I eagerly clutched it and tried to open it while asking the Lord for His help.

## JOSHUA 1:9

I did not personally open the Bible to Joshua 1:9. Struggling with it, it opened to this very verse of Scripture, and I know beyond the shadow of a doubt that it was the Lord who did it. He knew exactly what I needed.

The words of verse 9 seemed to be capitalized. They leaped up from the page, and I will never forget it: *"HAVE NOT I COMMANDED THEE? BE STRONG AND OF A GOOD COURAGE; BE NOT AFRAID, NEITHER BE THOU DISMAYED: FOR THE LORD THY GOD IS WITH THEE WHITHERSOEVER THOU GOEST."*

This was the word of the Lord to me. It was a word that has stuck with me from that day until now. The Lord was telling me, even as He had told Joshua so long, long ago, "I am commanding you." In other words, it doesn't matter how the situation looks; it doesn't matter about circumstances; and it doesn't matter about the present problems. Forget these things and *"be strong and of a good courage; be not afraid, neither be thou dismayed."*

The Lord was telling me to have faith in Him. He was telling me that I did not have anything to worry about. He was telling me that victory was mine if I would only believe it.

Then it said, *"FOR THE LORD THY GOD IS WITH YOU WHITHERSOEVER THOU GOEST."* I have stood on that word from then until now. There have been some dark days in the meantime; however, the Lord has never failed me, and I know that He never will!

## THE PRESENCE OF THE LORD

As the Lord gave me His word that night, His presence filled my heart and life as well. In fact, it literally filled that room. I remember thinking that I didn't have to stay in that bed any longer. With that, I gently placed my feet on the floor, arose, and started to walk, praising the Lord.

When Frances and Donnie came home that night about an hour or so later, Frances found me walking from room to room (the little house was small, only four rooms). I was doing so constantly, and I was praising the Lord. In other words, she left me sick and found me well and healed when she came back.

So, Joshua 1:9 means very much to me personally. As it was the Lord's word to Joshua, it was His word to me.

Oh yes, I realize the circumstances were altogether different. Joshua was responsible for an entire nation, while my small effort only concerned myself, yet, that's not quite right.

Because of what the Lord did for me that night, it helped me to touch this world for Christ in future years, literally seeing untold hundreds of thousands of souls being brought to the Lord Jesus Christ, and I exaggerate not.

As well, I believe that I have the authority of the Lord to say this to you who are reading these words: As it was the word of the Lord to Joshua, it was also the word of the Lord to me. I believe it is also the word of the Lord to you: *"Have not I commanded thee? Be strong and of a good courage; be not afraid, neither be thou dismayed: for the LORD thy God is with you whithersoever thou goest."*

Even as I dictate these words, I sense the presence of God, and I believe the Lord is speaking right now to my heart, saying to you: "As I was real to Joshua so long, long ago, and as I was real to you when you began your ministry those years ago, I will be just as real to you today and to anyone and everyone who will dare to believe My Word."

*"Then Joshua commanded the officers of the people, saying, Pass through the host, and command the people, saying, Prepare you victuals; for within three days ye shall pass over this Jordan, to go in to possess the land, which the LORD your God giveth you to possess it"* (Josh. 1:10-11).

## POSSESSING THE LAND

Israel could have possessed the land some thirty-eight years earlier had they only evidenced faith. However, unbelief caused them to languish in the wilderness for some thirty-eight extra years, in fact, until the generation above twenty years of age who had come out of Egypt died off.

There are far too many modern Christians who are languishing in a spiritual wilderness because of misplaced faith.

To inherit the promises of God, we must evidence faith in Christ and the cross, which will give the Holy Spirit latitude to work in our lives. He alone can help us to possess all that God has promised (I Cor. 1:17-18, 21, 23; 2:2).

To be factual, even blunt, unless one understands the cross of Christ not only relative to salvation, but, also for sanctification, one simply cannot have all that God wants him to have. I don't mean that it's difficult, hard, or out of the reach of most; I mean no one can be what he ought to be in Christ or do what he ought to do for Christ unless that person understands the message of the cross. It's just that simple, and at the same time, it's just that complicated.

Jesus Christ is the source of all things, while the cross is the means by which these things are given to us.

We do it God's way, which is the way of the cross, or we do not do it at all. It's the cross, the cross, the cross! Of course, we are speaking of what Jesus there did.

*And to the Reubenites, and to the Gadites, and to half the tribe of Manasseh, spake Joshua, saying, Remember the word which Moses the servant of the LORD commanded you, saying, The LORD your God hath given you rest, and hath given you this land. Your wives, your little ones, and your cattle, shall remain in the land which Moses gave you on this side Jordan; but ye shall pass before your brethren armed, all the mighty men of valour, and help them; Until the LORD have given your brethren rest, as he hath given you, and they also have possessed the land which the LORD your God giveth them: then ye shall return unto the land of your possession, and enjoy it, which Moses the LORD's servant gave you on this side Jordan toward the sunrising (Josh. 1:12-15).*

## REMEMBER THE WORD

Had the two tribes and the half tribe permitted God to choose for them, how much happier and safer they would have been! However, they chose for themselves land on the wrong side of Jordan and brought upon themselves many sorrows and early captivity (1 Kings 22:3).

Such is the sad experience of Christians who plan for themselves and do not have fellowship with the thoughts of God. God's plan was to conquer Canaan and then the land stretching from the Jordan to the Euphrates. The two tribes, the Reubenites and the Gadites, and the half tribe of Manasseh thought the reverse would be the better plan. It wasn't, even as man's plans are never the better plan, and I mean never!

## GOD'S WILL

As we've already stated, the Lord had a perfect plan for Israel. It was conceived in heaven, birthed in heaven, and planned in heaven. Everything was worked out by the Lord, even down to the smallest details. None of it was of man; all of it was of God.

However, the tribes of Reuben and Gad, along with the half tribe of Manasseh, were not satisfied with God's plans, but rather inserted their own.

They wanted now to occupy land on the eastern side of Jordan. Was this what the Lord had chosen for them? No! But it's what they wanted.

Man is very capable of making his own plans and then asking God to bless those plans. To be truthful, God can never really bless such. He may tolerate it, but unless He conceives the plans, gives birth to the plans, and then carries out the plans, they cannot be what they ought to be.

## THE PERFECT WILL OF GOD

Every believer should want nothing but the perfect will of God. If there is such a thing as a permissive will, we should not desire such but only God's perfect will. Only then is such guaranteed for blessings.

Paul said: "*Present your bodies a living sacrifice, holy, acceptable unto God, which is your reasonable service. And be not conformed to this world: but be you transformed by the renewing of your mind, that you may prove what is that good, and acceptable, and perfect, will of God*" (Rom. 12:1-2).

The idea is that the only will that is acceptable unto God is a perfect will. To be sure, the Lord alone has such!

As far as we know, the tribes of Reuben, Gad, and the half tribe of Manasseh were the first to go into captivity. The Scripture says of them: "*And they transgressed against the God of their fathers, and went a whoring after the gods of the people of the land, whom God destroyed before them. And the God of Israel stirred up the spirit of Pul king of Assyria, and the spirit of Tiglath-Pileser king of Assyria, and he carried them away, even the Reubenites, and the Gadites, and the half tribe of Manasseh*" (I Chron. 5:25-26).

The Holy Spirit is here quick to point out that it was these particular tribes who first lost their way. Even though it was approximately 150 years after their fathers had settled that part of the land, still, I personally believe that their getting out of the will of God those many long years before was what ultimately brought on their downfall, with all of its attendant misery.

While the mills of God may grind slowly, they always grind exceedingly fine, meaning they miss nothing.

*"And they answered Joshua, saying, All that you command us we will do, and wheresoever thou sendest us, we will go. According as we hearkened unto Moses in all things, so will we hearken unto thee: only the LORD thy God be with you, as He was with Moses. Whosoever he be that doth rebel against your commandment, and will not hearken unto thy words in all that thou commandest him, he shall be put to death: only be strong and of a good courage"* (Josh. 1:16-18).

## FAMOUS FIRST WORDS

Obedience is easy when all goes well with us and when it makes little demand upon our faith.

The worthlessness of man's promises of fidelity at the close of this chapter contrasts with the worthfulness of God's promises of faithfulness at the opening of these passages.

Verse 18 illustrates the disobedience and folly of the natural heart. Man is always willing to obey a human rather than a divine law.

These men, who now condemned to death any who refused to obey Joshua, themselves refused to obey Jehovah.

**OBEDIENCE?**

In response to Joshua's leadership, these individuals, who were the leaders of these respective tribes, seemed to say the right thing. In fact, they did say the right things; however, saying something and then doing it is quite different.

We must all know the period of struggle when we *"delight in the law of God after the inward man"* (Rom. 7:22), but find another law in our members at conflict with it. So must we learn to find the only deliverance from *"the body of this death"* (Rom. 7:24). It is always and without exception in Jesus Christ our Lord, with us exhibiting faith in Him and what He has done for us at the cross. There is no other deliverance (Rom. 6:1-14).

The truth is, despite our good intentions, we really cannot properly obey, even at this present time, and even under the new covenant, unless we seek to render obedience according to God's prescribed order.

**GOD'S PRESCRIBED ORDER OF VICTORY**

If we know this divine order, which is given to us in the Word of God, and faithfully attempt to obey it, we will find the help of the Holy Spirit, without whose help any progress is impossible. He, without reservation, will constantly come to our aid. In fact, we cannot really be anything for the Lord, do anything for the Lord, or have anything from the Lord unless it is given to us by the Holy Spirit. He alone is able to make us what we ought to be (I Cor. 3:16).

In brief, God's prescribed order of victory is that we understand Christ is the source of all things, and we speak of all things good, while the cross is the means, and the only means, of receiving all of these things. This means that every single thing we receive from God, and I mean everything, comes to us strictly from Christ but by and through the cross. Without the cross, we could not have anything from the Lord. The cross of Christ has made it all possible (I Cor. 1:17-18, 23; 2:2; Gal. 2:20-21; Gal., Chpt. 5; 6:14).

This means that our faith must be anchored constantly and consistently in the cross of Christ. If we fully believe that everything comes to us by the means of the cross (what Jesus there did), then it will be easy for us to anchor our faith there; however, if we vacillate as it regards the object of our faith being the cross, then we have problems.

With the cross of Christ being the object of our faith, the Holy Spirit will then begin to work mightily on our behalf. As previously stated, He alone can make us what we ought to be (Rom. 8:1-2, 11). It must ever be understood that the Holy Spirit works exclusively within the parameters of the finished work of Christ. In other words, what Jesus did at the cross gives the Holy Spirit the legal means to do all that He does with us, and that's why it is required that the cross of Christ ever be the object of our faith (Rom. 8:1-2, 11).

Any true Christian wants to live right, wants to do right, wants to be right, wants to bring forth fruit for the Lord, and wants to grow in grace and the knowledge of the Lord. In fact, that is an inbred spirit within the hearts and lives of all who are truly born again. Such a desire and such a hunger and thirst are placed there by the Holy Spirit in the realm of the divine nature. However, all of this can be obtained in only one way, and that is by and through Christ and what Christ has done for us at the cross and our faith in that ever present object.

## THE BIBLE IS THE STORY OF JESUS CHRIST AND HIM CRUCIFIED

The following will give us a brief summary of what the Bible is all about. If we understand it in this fashion, then we will understand it as we should. Actually, the first chapter of the gospel according to John spells it out.

The first verse tells us that the entirety of the Bible is about Jesus Christ.

John said, and I quote from The Expositor's Study Bible: "*In the beginning* (does not infer that Christ as God had a beginning because as God, He had no beginning, but rather refers to the time of creation [Gen. 1:1]) *was the Word* (the Holy Spirit through John describes Jesus as 'the eternal Logos'), *and the Word was with* God ('was in relationship with God,' and expresses the idea of the Trinity), *and the Word was God* (meaning that He did not cease to be God during the incarnation; He 'was' and 'is' God from eternity past to eternity future)" (John 1:1).

This one verse plainly and clearly tells us that Jesus Christ is God and that He is the eternal Word. So, this tells us that the entirety of the Bible is about Jesus Christ and, in fact, Jesus Christ and Him crucified (I Cor. 1:23).

## THE INCARNATION

Now verse 14 tells us why God became man. It says, *"And the Word was made flesh* (refers to the incarnation, 'God becoming man'), *and dwelt among us* (refers to Jesus, although perfect, not holding Himself aloft from all others, but rather lived as all men, even a peasant), *and we beheld His glory, the glory as of the only begotten of the Father,* (speaks of His deity, although hidden from the eyes of the merely curious; while Christ laid aside the expression of His deity, He never for a moment lost the possession of His deity) *full of grace and truth* (as 'flesh' proclaimed His humanity, 'grace and truth' His deity)" (John. 1:14).

And now, John 1:29 tells us why the eternal Word became flesh and dwelt among us: *"The next day* (refers to the day after John had been questioned by the emissaries from the Sanhedrin) *John sees Jesus coming unto him* (is, no doubt, after the baptism of Jesus and the temptation in the wilderness), *and said, Behold the Lamb of God* (proclaims Jesus as the sacrifice for sin, in fact, the sin offering, whom all the multiple millions of offered lambs had represented), *which takes away the sin of the world* (animal blood could only cover sin, it could not take it away; but Jesus offering Himself as the perfect sacrifice took away the sin of the world; He not only cleansed acts of sin, but, as well, addressed the root cause [Col. 2:14-15])" (John. 1:29) – The Expositor's Study Bible

So, in three verses of Scripture found in John 1, we find who Jesus is, what Jesus is, and what He did!

*Hast thou heard Him, seen Him, known Him?*
*Is not yours a captured heart?*
*Chief among ten thousand own Him,*
*Joyful choose the better part.*

*Idols once they won thee, charmed thee,*
*Lovely things of time and sense;*
*Gilded thus does sin disarm thee,*
*Honeyed lest you turn thee thence.*

*Tis that look that melted Peter,*
*Tis that face that Stephen saw,*
*Tis the heart that wept with Mary*
*Can alone from idols draw.*

# RAHAB
## AND OTHER
# MIRACLES

## THE PRECIOUS
## BLOOD OF CHRIST

# THE PRECIOUS BLOOD OF CHRIST

## THE FOUNDATION

The following passage gives us the foundation of the great redemption plan. Peter said:

> *Forasmuch as you know that you were not redeemed with corruptible things, as silver and gold* (presents the fact that the most precious commodities [silver and gold] could not redeem fallen man), *from your vain conversation* (vain lifestyle) *received by tradition from your fathers* (speaks of original sin that is passed on from father to child at conception); *But with the precious blood of Christ* (presents the payment, which proclaims the poured out life of Christ on behalf of sinners), *as of a lamb without blemish and without spot* (speaks of the lambs offered as substitutes in the old Jewish economy; the death of Christ was not an execution or assassination, but rather a sacrifice; the offering of Himself presented a perfect sacrifice, for He was perfect in every respect [Ex. 12:5]):

## FOREORDAINED

> *Who verily was foreordained before the foundation of the world* (refers to the fact that God, in His omniscience, knew He would create man, man would fall, and man would be redeemed by God becoming man in order to go to the cross; this was all done before the universe was created; this means the cross of Christ is the foundation doctrine of all doctrine, referring to the fact that all doctrine must be built upon that foundation, or else, it is specious), *but was manifest in these last times for you* (refers to the invisible God who, in the person of the Son, was made visible to human eyesight by assuming a human body and human limitations) (I Peter 1:18-20)
> – The Expositor's Study Bible

Purely and simply, this passage of Scripture tells us that the cross of Christ is the foundation of all that we have in the Lord. It was formulated by the Godhead, at least in the mind of the Godhead, even before the foundation of the world. This means, and this is very important, that every single doctrine in the Bible is built upon the foundation of the cross, and any doctrine that does not fit that category will conclude in error. In fact, that's the reason that the church presently is loaded down with false doctrine. It doesn't understand the cross, and in many cases, if not most, it doesn't even really believe in the cross; consequently, it is an open target for the powers of Satan.

If a doctrine is built squarely on the cross of Christ, then in some way, it will come out right. Otherwise, it will come out wrong.

## OLD TESTAMENT TYPOLOGY

All of the typology in the Old Testament pointed in some way to Christ in either His atoning, mediatorial, or intercessory work. This included the entirety of the sacrificial system, which was originated on the very first page of human history (Genesis 4). It, as well, included the entirety of the law of Moses. Everything about all of this, and I mean all of it, pointed to Christ.

Paul referred to all of the Old Testament economy as *"a shadow of things to come"* (Col. 2:17).

The great apostle also said:

> *But when the fulness of the time was come* (which completed the time designated by God that should elapse before the Son of God would come), *God sent forth His Son* (it was God who acted; the law required man to act; this requirement demonstrated man's impotency; the Son of God requires nothing from man other than his confidence), *made of a woman* (pertains to the incarnation, God becoming man), *made under the law* (refers to the Mosaic law; Jesus was subject to the Jewish legal economy, which He had to be, that is, if He was to redeem fallen humanity; in other words, He had to keep the law perfectly, which no human being had ever done, but He did), *To redeem them who were under the law* (in effect, all of humanity is under the law of God, which man, due to his fallen condition, could not keep; but Jesus came and redeemed us by keeping the law perfectly, and above all, satisfying its penalty upon the cross, which was

death), *that we might receive the adoption of sons* (that we could become the sons of God by adoption, which is carried out by faith in Christ and what He did for us at the cross) (Gal. 4:4-5) – The Expositor's Study Bible

As stated, everything under the Jewish law pointed to Christ, in effect, the cross, of which the entire sacrificial system was a type. When Israel began to leave the cross, so to speak, that's when they lost their way and went ultimately into captivity (Deut. 28).

The sacrificial system was the heart of the old Jewish system, and the sacrificial system in its entirety pointed to the cross, as should be overly obvious (Ex. 12:13).

## THE NEW COVENANT

The Old Testament was a pattern for the new covenant, which means that through typology, allegorical examples, illustrations, and examples, it pointed straight to Christ and the cross. As Israel looked forward to the coming Redeemer, we now look backward to the Redeemer who has already come.

In the Old Testament, they looked forward to a prophetic Jesus, while we look back to a historical Jesus. As the cross was the centerpiece of the old economy, which was symbolized by the sacrificial system, likewise, we now have the finished work, and it is all centered up in the cross of Christ.

Let us be blunt: If the church leaves the cross, it will destroy itself exactly as did Israel of old. In fact, the apostle Paul laid it out in no uncertain terms:

*For if God spared not the natural branches* (Israel), *take heed lest He also spare not you* (again refers to the church, as is obvious). *Behold therefore the goodness and severity of God* (don't mistake the goodness of God for license): *on them which fell, severity* (speaks of judgment which came on Israel, God's chosen people); *but toward you, goodness, if you continue in His goodness* (proclaims the condition; the continuing of that 'goodness' pertains to continued faith in Christ and the cross): *otherwise you also shall be cut off* (is the modern church on the edge of that even now? Revelation 3:15-22 tells us this, in fact, is the case!) (Rom. 11:21-22) – The Expositor's Study Bible

Therefore, it is the cross of Christ, or it is spiritual destruction! There is no in-between.

*"And Joshua the son of Nun sent out of Shittim two men to spy secretly, saying, Go view the land, even Jericho. And they went, and came into an harlot's house, named Rahab, and lodged there"* (Josh. 2:1).

## JERICHO

The following material regarding Rahab has already been given in another one of our books; however, it would be virtually impossible to fully tell the story of Joshua and to eliminate Rahab. So, even though the following regarding Rahab will be repetitious, at least as far as another volume is concerned, I feel it is absolutely necessary that it also be included here.

The house spoken of in the verse just given was an inn of sorts. The two spies did not know that Rahab was a harlot. As well, some have attempted to claim that Rahab had been forced into temple prostitution. However, the Greek text of Hebrews 11:31 proves that she was a common harlot.

The two spies serve no military purpose whatsoever. So, why did Joshua send them?

The Lord told him to do so because of Rahab, even though Joshua did not know or understand such at the time. The Lord knew that faith lodged in the heart of this woman, and God will go to any lengths to honor faith, even that of a harlot (Hebrews 11).

As well, in a sense, Rahab was a type of the church that will be raptured out before the great tribulation.

As far as I'm concerned, the story of Rahab is one of the most gracious and one of the most telling of the grace of God found in the entirety of the Word of God. It shows us the love of God, and coupled with the grace of God, we have here an unparalleled illustration. As we go forward, let it be a blessing to you, as I know it shall.

## JERICHO AND THE TWO SPIES

Let's look at Jericho: This city is one of the oldest in the world. It was already a city of antiquity by the time of Joshua. It probably derived its name from the moon-god Yarih.

Located at the northern extremity of the Dead Sea, it was the entrance to Canaan from the east. In fact, at the time of Joshua, it was a mighty fortress. It was known for commerce as well as for agriculture. The proximity to the Dead Sea made the citizens dealers in salt, bitumen, and sulfur. However, irrespective of the city itself in the natural, the spiritual implications involved present a tremendous lesson for us.

This was the entrance to the promised land, and it barred Israel's progress. Its conquest, at least in the natural, was impossible to Israel, for its walls were great and high. But yet, it had to be subdued. The spiritual implications involved present a tremendous lesson for us.

It is a type of Satan's fortresses, which he places in our path in order to keep us from the great things of God. In fact, we receive nothing from the Lord without us defeating the satanic forces of darkness in some way. So, in order to take the promised land, to have what God had promised them, and to enjoy this land of milk and honey, Jericho first had to be subdued. Is there a Jericho hindering your progress? Is there a Jericho keeping you from having that which the Lord has promised you? Is there a Jericho that stands in your way?

As we go forward in our study, we will see God's way, and we will find out that this is the only way that victory can be brought about. Unfortunately, all too often, Christians attempt to gain victories by the means of the flesh, which can never happen. It can only be done by the power of the Holy Spirit.

## WHAT IS THE FLESH?

The flesh pertains to that which is indigenous to a human being. In other words, it is our personal talents, education, motivation, ability, etc. It is whatever a human being can do.

These things are not sin within themselves, but whatever it is that we need in the spiritual sense, we cannot gain it by those means, no matter the strength of our willpower. It cannot be done. God's way is the cross of Christ and, in fact, it is His only way. When the believer evidences faith in Christ and the cross, then the Holy Spirit will begin to work within his heart and life and do what He alone can do. To be sure, the Holy Spirit, who is God, can do anything. However, at the same time, He will not function as He desires unless our faith is properly placed, and the proper placement of our faith is the cross of Christ.

## WHY THE CROSS?

It is there where Jesus defeated every power of darkness, and He did so by atoning for all sin—past, present, and future—at least for all who will believe (John 3:16; I Cor. 1:17-18, 23; 2:2; Col. 2:10-15; Rom. 8:1-11). That is God's way, and the terrible sin of the church is spiritual adultery.

## WHAT IS SPIRITUAL ADULTERY?

Every person who has accepted Christ as his Savior and Lord, in effect, is married to the Lord (II Cor. 11:1-4; Rom. 7:1-4). Being married to Christ, He will meet, and desires to meet, our every need. For those needs to be met, our faith must be exclusively in Christ and the cross. When we place our faith in something else, we, in effect, are being unfaithful to Christ. This means that we are committing spiritual adultery, and it causes the same problem in the spirit world as natural adultery does in the physical world. And yet, sad to say, by not understanding the cross of Christ relative to sanctification, most Christians are living in a state of spiritual adultery. One can well imagine how this hinders the Holy Spirit. Thank God that He doesn't leave us in such circumstances, but it does cause great problems, and those problems can cause us tremendous trouble.

God's way is simple. It is actually Jesus Christ and Him cruci-fied. In effect, and in short, that is the gospel. In fact, the entirety of the Bible from Genesis 1:1 through Revelation 22:21 is the story of Jesus Christ and Him crucified. As stated, this is God's way, and He will never have another way. The reason is simple: His way works.

That's the reason the material we are now giving you is so very, very important. In fact, it is the difference in victory and defeat. The only way we're going to defeat the Jerichos in our hearts and lives is that we place our faith in the correct object, which is the cross of Christ. Otherwise, those fortresses will defeat us.

## THE TWO SPIES

There was absolutely no military reason for Joshua to send two spies to Jericho in order to spy out the land. This battle would not be fought by natural means anyway, so whatever information they brought back, at least as it regarded military information, would be useless. So, it must have been that the Lord impressed upon Joshua to send in these two men.

I think it can only be concluded that Rahab was the reason for their being sent. Even though this woman was a vile sinner, which we will deal with momentarily, still, evidence is that a cry of faith was in her soul. That cry of faith would be answered by the Lord, as every cry of faith is always answered by the Lord.

I do not think it would be a stretch of the imagination to portray what happened at Jericho to be a portent of that which is soon to happen in this world. We speak of the soon coming great tribulation, and above all, the rapture of the church.

Considering the entirety of the population of the city, whatever it may have been, Rahab and her family were the only ones spared. As well, considering the entirety of the population of the world, which presently stands at approximately 7.8 billion people, the number of people who are truly born again at this time, and who will make the rapture, is truly small. So, Rahab definitely could be a type of the church that will be delivered out of the coming judgment.

## OBEY THE WORD

The only way that Rahab and her family could be spared was by adhering totally to what they were told by the two spies. They were not to question it, not to add to it, and were not to take from it. Their lives, their souls, and everything they had depended totally and completely upon what the two spies related to them. It is the same, presently, with the Word of God on which the Holy Spirit works exclusively.

If Rahab had changed the instructions in any way, she would have never been spared. I'm afraid that much of the modern church presently is most definitely attempting to change the instructions. The Word of God is being replaced presently with religious books that refer to themselves as bibles, and I speak of those such as *The Message Bible,* etc., but which, in reality, are not bibles at all. How do I know?

These are thought-for-thought translations, even at that, which can never pass scriptural and spiritual muster. If you as a believer do not have a word-for-word translation, such as the King James Version, then you really don't have a bible. I would strongly recommend for you to get for yourselves a copy of The Expositor's Study Bible. It is King James, but it explains virtually every Scripture, with the explanation embedded within the Scripture. It is one of the best-selling study bibles in the world today, and to be sure, your money will not be wasted.

**THE KING JAMES BIBLE**

Some counter that by saying, "I can't understand the King James".

First of all, if you have something that you can understand, and it's actually not the Word of God, you have not done yourself any good whatsoever. In fact, you have done yourself irreparable harm. A road map that is wrong will never lead one to the right destination. Blueprints that are faulty will never build a house that will stand. Jesus said so (Mat. 7:24-27)!

The Holy Spirit functions entirely on, within, and by the Word of God. In fact, He is the author of the Word. Peter said: *"For the prophecy* (the word *prophecy* is used here in a general sense, covering the entirety of the Word of God, which means it's not limited merely to predictions regarding the future) *came not in old time by the will of man* (did not originate with man): *but holy men of God spoke as they were moved by the Holy Spirit.* (This proclaims the manner in which the Word of God was written and, thereby, given unto us)" (II Peter 1:21).

Actually, I have just given you an example of how The Expositor's Study Bible is put together. As stated, it will help you to understand the Word, I think, as nothing that's ever been placed in your hands. We strongly advise every believer to get a copy.

Remember this: We aren't speaking here from a position of personal preference, but rather that which pertains to eternal consequences. If the Word of God is misinterpreted, the person will die eternally lost. So, considering the implications and considering the eternal consequences, I think it would certainly be wise for every believer to *"make your* (his) *calling and election sure"* (II Peter 1:10).

The idea is that if it's not the pure Word of God, meaning that which has not been compromised, then the Holy Spirit, without whom we receive nothing, will not, and, in fact, cannot function. He functions alone and entirely on and in the Word of God.

So, if we want the moving and operation of the Holy Spirit within our hearts and lives, we had better make certain that we truly have the Word of God in our possession, and not some hybrid.

## RAHAB

George Williams said concerning Rahab:

> Rahab was a debauched member of a doomed race. Yet, grace saved her. She based her plea for salvation upon the fact that she was justly ordained by God to destruction. Many people refuse to bestir themselves in the matter of personal salvation because of the belief that if they are ordained to be saved, they will be saved, and if ordained to be lost, they will be lost, which constitutes an erroneous interpretation of predestination. All sinners are justly ordained to be lost (Rom. 5:12), and, therefore, all sinners may be saved. Rahab prefaced her plea for salvation by declaring that she knew all were doomed to destruction, and because of this divine judgment, she asked for a true token that would assure her of her safety in the day of wrath that was coming.[1]

## THE WAY OF SALVATION

Rahab was immediately provided with a way of salvation. It was a very simple way, something that anyone could do. She had but to bind a scarlet cord in a window. A child could do that. Salvation today from the wrath to come is equally simple.

Trusting in the Lord Jesus Christ and in His precious blood secures eternal salvation.

Williams continues, "Rahab lost not a moment in making her calling and election sure. She bound the scarlet cord in the window. And directly she did so, she was saved—that is, she was in safety, and assured of safety. Prior to binding the scarlet line in the window, she was ordained to destruction, but the moment she trusted that 'true token,' she was ordained to salvation."[2]

## THE ASSURANCE OF SALVATION

Rahab's assurance of salvation was not founded upon an inward experience but upon an outward evidence—that is, the scarlet cord. It was perfection, but in herself, imperfection. By looking upon that true token and believing the testimony respecting it, she was assured deliverance on the day of doom that was coming. Thus, the outward token gave an inward peace. The believer in Jesus enjoys a similar peace. The preciousness of Christ's blood and the testimony of the Holy Scriptures concerning it are the outward tokens, which bring assurance of salvation to the heart that trusts Christ. It was vain for Rahab to seek for salvation upon the grounds of personal worthiness, for she was vile indeed. It is equally vain for the most moral to claim salvation today, for all have sinned, none are righteous, and all are under sentence of death (Rom. 5:12).

Williams continues: "A faith that is born of God always evidences itself by seeking the salvation of others. Rahab pleads for her father, her mother, her brothers, her sisters, and all belonging to them; and they were all saved. The moral effect of a divine faith is further seen in Rahab. She became a good woman, and joined the people of God, married one of its princes, and her name shines in the genealogy of Jesus Christ (Matt. 1:5)."[3]

## THE KING OF JERICHO

> *And it was told the king of Jericho, saying, Behold, there came men in hither tonight of the children of Israel to search out the country. And the king of Jericho sent unto Rahab, saying, Bring forth the men who are come to thee, which are entered into thine house: for they be come to search out all the country. And the woman took the two men, and hid them, and said thus, There came men unto me, but I wist not whence they were: And it came to pass about the time of shutting of the gate, when it was dark, that the men went out: where the men went I wot know: pursue after them quickly; for ye shall overtake them. But she had brought them up to the roof of the house, and hid them with the stalks of flax, which she had laid in order upon the roof. And the men pursued after them the way to Jordan unto the fords: and as soon as they which pursued after them were gone out, they shut the gate (Josh. 2:2-7).*

We know from the scriptural narrative that Rahab lied to the two men sent to her by the king as it regarded the two spies.

The sacred historian simply narrates the fact and makes no comment whatever upon it.

The roofs of houses, then as now, were flat in those regions. She hid the men on the roof under stalks of flax. The germ of faith was already stirring in her heart, and it was faith that would be amply rewarded. We must not judge Rahab, for all of this was shortly before her conversion. To be sure, we must not judge Rahab at all.

Despite her past, this woman would go down in biblical history as one of the greatest women of God ever. In fact, she would be in the genealogy of Christ, and nothing could be greater than that (Matt. 1:5).

## FAITH

Faith begins in the heart of the sinner, placed there by the Holy Spirit even before conversion. In fact, it has to begin before conversion, or there could be no conversion.

What was it that stirred this woman's heart to begin with, especially considering the lifestyle she was leading as a harlot?

At that time, and with over two million Israelites camped on the other side of Jordan, the entirety of the city was abuzz with these proceedings. It seems from what Rahab would say momentarily that all the victories of the recent past regarding Israel were well known in Jericho. Also, Israel's deliverance from Egypt and the opening of the waters of the Red Sea were all well known, despite the fact that this took place nearly forty years before.

## JEHOVAH

It would seem that from this, in some way, faith began to build in the heart of this woman. In those days, everything was attributed to the god of the particular people or country involved; consequently, it was known that the God of Israel must be stronger than the many gods of Egypt because Egypt had been left a wreck upon the deliverance of these people. As well, it would have been deduced that Jehovah was greater than the gods of the Amorites, etc. Therefore, whatever was said, or whatever was deduced from all of this, faith began to build in the heart of Rahab, on which the Holy Spirit worked.

At that time, the knowledge of the victories of Israel would have been constituted as the Word of the Lord. The Holy Spirit always works on the Word, or else, He doesn't work. If something is preached behind the pulpit that's not the Word, the Holy Spirit will not work. It is the Word of God alone on which He functions, ever how that Word is presented. As stated, this would have only been a story that was related, but yet, true.

While the entirety of the city was rife with all of this information, still, it was Rahab alone and her family who chose to believe in the God of Israel. Quite possibly this dear lady was sick of her supposed god, Chemosh, which she had been worshipping. It was rather common for little children to be offered up to this god as a burnt offering, which was carried on quite often. No doubt this sickened Rahab, with what little she knew about Jehovah striking a positive chord in her heart. At any rate, it would lead to her salvation and a place in biblical history that is all out of proportion to mere human thought. The story of Rahab cannot be said to be anything but a story of faith. It is faith that believed God, and such faith is always honored and recognized.

## WE HAVE HEARD

> *And before they were laid down, she came up unto them upon the roof; And she said unto the men, I know that the LORD hath given you the land, and that your terror is fallen upon us, and that all the inhabitants of the land faint because of you. For we have heard how the LORD dried up the water of the Red Sea for you, when ye came out of Egypt; and what ye did unto the two kings of the Amorites, who were on the other side Jordan, Sihon and Og, whom ye utterly destroyed. And as soon as we had heard these things, our hearts did melt, neither did there remain any more courage in any man, because of you: for the LORD your God, He is God in heaven above, and in earth beneath* (Josh. 2:8-11).

Rahab's faith is shown by the expression, *"has given."* What God willed, she regarded as already done.

Bearing in mind the circumstances of the person who uttered it, the declaration of verse 11 is as remarkable as Peter's, *"Thou art the Christ, the Son of the living God"* (Matt. 16:16-17). Upon the utterance of this statement of faith, Rahab was saved, which was evidenced in her obedience regarding the true token (the red cord).

## THE TRUE TOKEN

> *Now therefore, I pray you, swear unto me by the* LORD, *since
> I have shewed you kindness, that ye will also shew kindness
> unto my father's house, and give me a true token: And that
> ye will save alive my father, and my mother, and my brethren,
> and my sisters, and all that they have, and deliver our lives
> from death. And the men answered her, Our life for yours, if
> ye utter not this our business. And it shall be, when the* LORD
> *hath given us the land, that we will deal kindly and truly with
> thee. Then she let them down by a cord through the window:
> for her house was upon the town wall, and she dwelt upon the
> wall. And she said unto them, Get you to the mountain, lest the
> pursuers meet you; and hide yourselves there three days, until
> the pursuers be returned: and afterward may you go your way*
> (Josh. 2:12-16).

From the conversation of Rahab, it is evident that all of the
surrounding nations knew of the tremendous miracles performed by Jehovah in Egypt, and especially the waters of the
Red Sea drying up for passage by the Israelites. Also, she was
very well acquainted with recent victories pertaining to Sihon
and Og.

In hearing these accounts discussed over and over, which
they were, the story of these great victories ignited a spark
of faith in the heart of this poor woman. She knew little of
Jehovah; however, she knew enough to know that Jehovah
was greater and stronger than all of the gods of Egypt, etc.

Upon that fact, she was in the process of making some decisions within her heart.

Knowing and seeing the heart of this dear lady, the Holy Spirit would move favorably upon her faith, which He had tendered her way in the first place. This is true irrespective of her debauched occupation, irrespective of the terrible vice that gripped her, and irrespective of what had transpired in the past.

## WHY RAHAB AND NOT OTHERS IN JERICHO?

It has ever been in that fashion. Many hear the gospel, but only a minute few accept the gospel. As to exactly what causes most to say no and some few to say yes is known only to God. This we do know: God does not tamper with the free moral agency of mankind. He will move upon people, deal with people, speak to people, and bring events to pass to impress people, but He will never force the issue. The decision must be, whether yes or no, that of the individual.

But yet, as we see the Word of God, we know it is imperative that all be given an opportunity, whatever their decision. The Holy Spirit is insistent upon that. Jesus Himself said:

> *Go ye into all the world* (the gospel of Christ is not merely a Western gospel, as some claim, but is for the entirety of the world), *and preach the gospel to every creature* ('preaching' is God's method, as is here plainly obvious; as well, it is imperative that every single person have the opportunity

to hear; this is the responsibility of every believer). *He who believes* (believes in Christ and what He did for us at the cross) *and is baptized* (baptized into Christ, which is done by faith [Rom. 6:3-5], not water baptism) *shall be saved; but he who believes not shall be damned* [John 3:16]) (Mark 16:15-16) – The Expositor's Study Bible

## WATER BAPTISM?

If Jesus had been speaking of water baptism in this verse, He then would have also said, "But he who believes not, and is not baptized in water, shall be damned." However, He didn't say that, but rather *"he who believes."*

The words of the Great Commission given in Matthew are a little different because the emphasis is different. Jesus said:

Go ye therefore (applies to any and all who follow Christ, and in all ages), *and teach all nations* (should have been translated, 'and preach to all nations,' for the word 'teach' here refers to a proclamation of truth), *baptizing them in the name of the Father, and of the Son, and of the Holy Spirit* (presents the only formula for water baptism given in the Word of God): *Teaching them* (means to give instruction) to observe all things (the whole gospel for the whole man) *whatsoever I have commanded you* (not a suggestion): *and, lo, I am with you always* (it is I, myself, God, and man, who am—not 'will be'—hence, forever present among you, and with you as companion, friend, guide, Savior, God), *even unto the end of the world* (should have been translated 'age'). *Amen* (it is the guarantee of My promise) (Matt. 28:19-20). – The Expositor's Study Bible

## THE SCARLET CORD

Upon the request of Rahab, the way of salvation was immediately made clear and plain to her. It was a very simple way. All she had to do was to hang a piece of scarlet cloth in the window. A child could do that. As well, salvation presently from the wrath to come is equally as simple. Trusting in the Lord Jesus Christ and in His precious blood, of which the scarlet cord was a type, secures eternal salvation.

As previously stated, the assurance of salvation in Rahab was not built upon an inward experience, but rather upon an outward evidence—that is, the scarlet cord. In it was perfection; in herself, imperfection. By looking upon that true token and believing the testimony respecting it, she was assured deliverance at the day of doom that was coming. Thus, the outward token gave an inward peace.

The believer in Jesus enjoys a similar peace. The preciousness of Christ's blood and the testimony of the Holy Scriptures concerning it are the outward tokens that bring assurance of salvation to the heart that trusts Christ.

It was vain for Rahab to seek for salvation upon the grounds of personal worthiness, for she was vile indeed. It is equally vain for the most moral to claim salvation today, for all have sinned, none are righteous, and all are under sentence of death (Rom. 5:12).

## THE COLOR OF BLOOD

The condition was that the red cord would hang from the window, and that all must stay in the house where the window was. To leave the house would be to leave its protection. Safety was guaranteed for all who remained in the house, but destruction for all who left the house. It is the same with the blood of Christ, which the scarlet cord represented.

As long as we remain in the house of safety provided by the blood, we are safe. To leave this house of safety, which is faith in Christ and Him crucified, guarantees destruction.

Scarlet, or rather crimson, is the color of blood. Like the blood on the doorposts in Egypt, it was to be the sign that the destroying messengers of God's vengeance were to respect and pass by. That scarlet cord alone could ensure safety, and it could ensure the safety only of those who trusted in it alone. It must be taken, therefore, as the type of salvation through the blood of Christ alone.

Let the reader understand that the only means of salvation is faith and trust in Christ and what He did for us at the cross, where He there shed His life's blood in order that we might be saved. The Scripture says: *"But now in Christ Jesus* (proclaims the basis of all salvation) *you who sometimes* (times past) *were far off* (far from salvation) *are made nigh* (near) *by the blood of Christ.* (The sacrificial atoning death of Jesus Christ transformed the relations of God with mankind. In Christ, God reconciled not a person, not even a nation, but rather 'a world' to Himself [II Cor. 5:19])" (Eph. 2:13) – The Expositor's Study Bible

## WHY IS THE BLOOD, OF WHICH THE SCARLET CORD WAS A TYPE, SO IMPORTANT?

We are speaking here of life and death and all of its implications. So, the Scripture says, *"For the life of the flesh is in the blood"* (Lev. 17:11).

As it regards payment for sin, God demanded life in payment, but it had to be a perfect life, which would necessitate perfect blood. No human being could do that simply because the fall had poisoned the entirety of the human race for all time.

So, in order to circumvent this terrible problem of the fall, God would become man, would have a special body prepared for Him, and would be born of the Virgin Mary. This would bypass, so to speak, the results of the fall. His body was perfect, and due to being virgin born, His blood was perfect. In fact, Simon Peter referred to it as *"precious blood"* (1 Peter 1:19).

When Christ hung on the cross, shedding His life's perfect blood, which came from a perfect body and a perfect life, God accepted this poured out life as total payment for all sin—past, present, and future—at least for all who will believe (John 3:16).

## ATONEMENT FOR SIN

In fact, every animal offered in sacrifice in Old Testament times, at least according to the directions of the Lord, was to be a substitute for the one who was to come, namely, the Lord Jesus Christ (Gen. 4). So the blood is important, but only as it is the blood of our Lord and Savior, Jesus Christ.

It is supremely important, but only as it was shed for you and me, which it was at the cross of Calvary. When He poured out His life, this atoned for all sin, as stated, past, present, and future (Rom. 3:22).

Regrettably and sadly, the modern church is dispensing with the cross, which means they are dispensing with the blood, which means they are dispensing with salvation. As stated, the cross of Christ is the only thing that stands between man and eternal hell. As well, the cross of Christ is the only thing that stands between the church and total apostasy.

## AND SHE BOUND A SCARLET LINE IN THE WINDOW

*And she said, According unto your words, so be it. And she sent them away, and they departed: and she bound the scarlet line in the window. And they went, and came unto the mountain, and abode there three days, until the pursuers were returned: and the pursuers sought them throughout all the way, but found them not. So the two men returned, and descended from the mountain, and passed over, and came to Joshua the son of Nun, and told him all things that befell them: And they said unto Joshua, Truly the LORD hath delivered into our hands all the land; for even all the inhabitants of the country do faint because of us (Josh. 2:21-24).*

Rahab lost not a moment in making her calling and election sure. She bound the scarlet line in the window and as she did so, she was saved—that is, she was in safety and assured of safety.

Prior to binding the scarlet line in the window, she was ordained to destruction, but from the moment she trusted that true token, she was ordained to salvation. As well, all of her family was ordained to salvation, provided they stayed in the house, which means that they placed their trust in the scarlet line also.

The report of the two spies, as it was given to Joshua, was one of faith, which was totally unlike the report that had been given some thirty-eight years earlier, which doomed a generation to die in the wilderness (Num. 13).

## THE GOOD REPORT

The report of the two spies was that already their enemies were disheartened and dispirited at the thought of the great name Jehovah, under the protection of which the Israelites fought.

Concerning this, Pulpit says, "So does the faithful soldier of Christ ever become a source of encouragement to his brethren. He who trusts in the Lord, and goes steadfastly about his work, never fails to find the enemies of the Lord fainting because of His soldiers. It is only the cowardly and distrustful who find the 'children of Anak,' and 'cities walled up to heaven' – that is insuperable difficulties and tasks beyond their powers. They who sit themselves in earnest to combat the enemies of God will neither make a compact with him nor be 'afraid of their faces,' are sure of victory. Sometimes the walls of some fortress of sin will fall as if by a miracle. Sometimes the enemy will only be discomfited after the prolonged and exhausting effort of a battle of Beth-horon. But the servants of God on the eve of a new conflict with the powers of evil may safely address their fellow warriors in the words, 'Truly the Lord has delivered into our hands all the land.'"[4]

## VICTORY

The child of God is to never think anything but victory. In fact, with the Lord leading Joshua and the children of Israel, irrespective of the forces against them, they simply could not lose. Who is able to stand up against Jehovah? Who is able to overcome Him? Who is able to discomfit Him? Of course, the entire world joined together could not overcome the Lord. We fight under His banner! We face Satan and his cohorts, not in our own strength, but rather in His strength.

The truth is, the victory was won at Calvary some two thousand years ago. It is not a conflict that is in doubt but a conflict that has already been fought and won.

Admittedly, Satan has been allowed to continue since that time, but only under the strict supervision of the Lord. In other words, the Evil One can do nothing except the Lord gives him permission to do so (Job 1-2).

*O I want to see him, look upon his face,*
*There to sing forever of his saving grace;*
*On the streets of Glory let me lift my voice;*
*Cares all past, home at last, ever to rejoice.*

# RAHAB
## AND OTHER
# MIRACLES

## TOMORROW THE LORD
## WILL DO WONDERS
## AMONG YOU

# TOMORROW THE LORD WILL DO WONDERS AMONG YOU

## WHY HAS THE LORD ALLOWED SATAN TO CONTINUE?

Considering that the Evil One was totally defeated at Calvary, that is a good question (Col. 2:14-15). However, believe it or not, Satan is not the problem of the believer. Satan has been allowed to continue in order for us to attain sanctification. We need an adversary that we might grow in grace and the knowledge of the Lord, that we might grow in faith and trust, and that we might learn to use our faith, and to use it as required.

The great problem of the believer is the problem of *self*. In other words, self is our biggest enemy. What do we mean by that?

First of all, we are "a self", and we will always be "a self". So, when a person comes to Christ, that individual does not cease to be "a self".

## THE PROBLEM OF SELF

I will first give the answer to the self problem. Jesus Himself gave us the means and the way of victory as it regards this difficulty. He said, *At that day* (after the resurrection and the coming of the Holy Spirit on the day of Pentecost) *you shall know that I am in My Father* (speaks of deity; Jesus is God!)*, and you in Me* (has to do with our salvation by faith)*, and I in you* (enables us to live a victorious life [Gal. 2:20]) (John 14:20) – The Expositor's Study Bible.

Self is safe only when it is hidden totally and completely in Christ.

The great problem with self is that it seeks to depend on its own strength, its own power, its own intellectualism, its own ability, etc., instead of depending solely and totally upon Christ and what Christ has done at the cross. This is the great battleground for the Christian. This is what Paul was talking about when he said, *"For the flesh* (in this case, evil desires) *lusteth against the spirit* (is the opposite of the Holy Spirit)*, and the Spirit against the flesh* (it is the Holy Spirit alone who can subdue the flesh; He does so, as we have repeatedly stated, by our faith being placed exclusively in Christ and the cross)*: and these are contrary the one to the other* (these two can never harmonize; as Paul has stated, the old nature must be cast out, which the Holy Spirit alone can do)*: so that you cannot do the things that you would.* (Without the Holy Spirit, who works by the cross, the believer cannot live a holy life)*"* (Gal. 5:17) – The Expositor's Study Bible

## THE HOLY SPIRIT

Some claim that the name or word *Spirit,* as given in this verse, is not the Holy Spirit, but rather the human spirit; however, when we look at the entirety of the chapter, we know that Paul is speaking of the Holy Spirit and not the spirit of man. For instance, he said in Galatians 5:18, *"But if you be led of the Spirit, you are not under the law."* He then went on to talk about the *"fruit of the Spirit"* in Galatians 5:22-23. So, the entire associating text in Galatians is speaking of the Holy Spirit and not the spirit of the individual.

As well, *Young's Literal Translation of the Holy Bible,* which does so from the Greek text, proclaims the fact that Paul is speaking here of the Holy Spirit.

## WHAT IS THE DIFFERENCE IN THE FLESH AND SELF?

One might say that the flesh is the ability of self. It is all the things that we can do as a human being of our own strength and intellectualism, whatever that might be. Within itself, there is really nothing wrong with that; however, the idea as given through Paul by the Holy Spirit, is that what needs to be done in the heart and life of the believer cannot be carried out by the flesh, i.e., our own strength and ability. It just simply cannot be done that way, but why?

Paul said, *"And if Christ be in you, the body is dead because of sin; but the Spirit is life because of righteousness"* (Rom. 8:10).

The passage means that the physical body has been rendered helpless because of the fall; consequently, the believer trying to overcome by willpower or any other means of the flesh presents a fruitless task. Only the Holy Spirit can make us what we ought to be, which means we cannot do it ourselves. He is God, and that means that He can do anything. For us to have His divine help, we only have to place our faith in Christ and the cross, and maintain it in Christ and the cross. Then the work will be done, and it's the only way that it will be done.

However, it is hard for the human being to admit this. Even if we do admit it, we will turn around and continue to try to bring to pass in our lives that which can only be accomplished by the Spirit.

## THE CARNAL MIND

Let me say it again: For everything and anything that we must have done within our hearts and lives as believers to make us what we ought to be (and I'm speaking of being done by the Lord), there is no way that we within ourselves can bring these things to pass. No matter how hard we try and no matter the effort we put forth, it cannot be done. Paul also said:

> *For to be carnally minded is death* (this doesn't refer to watching too much television as some think, but rather it's trying to live for God outside of His prescribed order; the results will be sin and separation from God); *but to be spiritually minded is life and peace* (God's prescribed order is the cross; this demands our constant faith in that finished work, which is the way of the Holy Spirit). *Because the carnal mind is enmity against God* (once again, this refers to attempting to live for God by means other than the cross, which places one 'against God'): *for it is not subject to the law of God, neither indeed can be* (in its simplest form means

that what is being done, whatever it may be, it's not in God's prescribed order, which is the cross). *So then they that are in the flesh cannot please God* (refers to the believer attempting to live his Christian life by means other than faith in Christ and the cross) (Rom. 8:6-8) – The Expositor's Study Bible

This is the great problem of the church and, in fact, the great problem of the believer.

## GOD'S PRESCRIBED ORDER OF VICTORY

Please note the following very carefully. We have placed it in abbreviated order, hopefully making it very easy to understand. This is God's prescribed order of victory; He has no other simply because no other is needed:

- Jesus Christ is the source of all things that we receive from God (Rom. 6:1-14; I Cor. 1:17-18, 23; 2:2).
- While our Lord is the source, the cross of Christ is the means by which all of these wonderful things are given to us. Please understand that the cross of Christ is not one of the means, but it is the only means (Col. 2:10-15; Gal. 6:14).
- With Christ as our source and the cross as our means, the object of our faith (and this is so very, very important) must ever be *"Jesus Christ, and Him crucified,"* i.e., the cross (I Cor. 1:17-18, 23; 2:2; Col. 2:10-15).
- With Christ as our source and the cross as the means, and the cross of Christ ever the object of our faith, then the

Holy Spirit will help us grandly. The Holy Spirit is God, and He works exclusively within the parameters of the cross of Christ, meaning that this is what gives Him the legal means to do all that He does (Rom. 8:1-11; Eph. 2:13-18).

*"And Joshua rose early in the morning; and they removed from Shittim, and came to Jordan, he and all the children of Israel, and lodged there before they passed over"* (Josh. 3:1).

## PREPARATIONS TO CROSS OVER

The evidence is that at this particular time, the Lord had not told Joshua exactly how they would pass over Jordan, just that it would be done. The Jordan River is normally only about fifty to one hundred feet wide; however, during the spring of every year, due to the rain, it would flood until it was approximately a mile and a half wide, at least as it ran near Jericho, and was at that time about forty feet deep. It doesn't do that now because so much water is siphoned out of the river to irrigate crops.

The crossing of the Jordan is a type of the baptism with the Holy Spirit, with deliverance from Egypt being a type of salvation.

Shittim was approximately ten miles due east of the Jordan River. Evidently this was where the children of Israel were camped.

The word *Shittim* means "a place of the wood, and with scourging thorns." In essence, it was a type of the wilderness experience and would be their last camping place before crossing the Jordan. In other words, the wilderness experience was about over.

Some have concluded that the crossing of the Jordan was the same thing as dying and going to heaven; however, the promised land, which was supposed to be a type of heaven, as we will find, was filled with enemies. There are no enemies in heaven; therefore, the promised land was not a type of heaven as some teach. It was rather a type of the baptism with the Holy Spirit.

## A BAPTISM OF POWER

To be sure, when one is baptized with the Holy Spirit, Satan then knows that such a person can now be of extreme danger to him and his kingdom of darkness. He will do all within his power to oppose such a child of God. To be sure, we now have the means to win the victory in every capacity; however, we come back to the age old problem of the flesh and self. As stated, the flesh is the means by which self attempts to carry forth its design. It is the greatest hindrance to the Holy Spirit.

The deliverance from Egypt is a type of salvation, and the wilderness experience is a type of refusing the baptism with the Holy Spirit and the cross of Christ as it regards our sanctification experience. If, in fact, that is a true statement, and it is, then for those who walk this particular path of disobedience, the situation becomes dire indeed! If the believer doesn't go on and be baptized with the Holy Spirit, considering the whole, precious few are going to make it. In fact, every single person who was delivered out of Egypt from twenty years old and upward died in the wilderness, with the exception of Joshua and Caleb. They, in effect, evidenced faith, and the Lord accredited to them entrance into the promised land, which they would now experience.

## THE BAPTISM WITH THE HOLY SPIRIT

The great prophet Joel prophesied and, thereby, predicted the *"former rain"* and the *"latter rain"* (Joel 2:23). This speaks of the outpouring of the Holy Spirit.

The former rain took place from the day of Pentecost throughout the early church, a time frame of approximately one hundred years. The church then began to apostatize, finally degenerating into what is now known as the Catholic Church. In fact, the Catholic Church came into being over several hundreds of years. It was a gradual process.

In the early days of the sixth century when the Catholic Church finally began to exert total control, the world was then plunged into the Dark Ages. You can lay that on the doorstep of the apostatizing of the church. The world did not come out of those Dark Ages until the Reformation, which came about in the 1400s.

At approximately the turn of the twentieth century, the latter rain outpouring commenced. Since that time, it is said that more than 500 million people have been baptized with the Holy Spirit with the evidence of speaking with other tongues (Acts 2:4).

## THE LIGHT

The Lord is very patient with His people. For instance, during the Dark Ages, when very little gospel of any nature was preached, the Lord dealt with the people according to the light they then had. Don't misunderstand; there had to be a modicum of faith, and that faith had to register in Christ in order for people to be saved because there is no other way that one can be saved. However, as is understood, precious few were actually saved during the Dark Ages simply because there was precious little gospel being preached. There was some, but not much.

However, once the light of the Reformation began to spread around the world, then the Spirit baptism began to be poured out upon hungry hearts. Inasmuch as light was given, in fact, more light than believers had had since the former rain, the Lord then expected, and now expects, much more of those who are saved. If believers presently reject the baptism with the Holy Spirit, which is always accompanied by speaking with other tongues as the Spirit of God gives the utterance, it presents itself as a serious thing indeed! If light is given, and light is rejected, I think the Scripture plainly tells us that what little light that was formerly had will be taken away and given to those who have accepted the light, whatever that light might be (Matt. 25:14-30).

## THE ARK OF THE COVENANT

*"And it came to pass after three days, that the officers went through the host; And they commanded the people, saying, When ye see the*

*ark of the covenant of the* LORD *your God, and the priests the Levites bearing it, then ye shall remove from your place, and go after it. Yet there shall be a space between you and it, about two thousand cubits by measure: come not near unto it, that ye may know the way by which ye must go: for ye have not passed this way heretofore"* ( Josh. 3:2-4).

The ark of the covenant was the dwelling place of God in His journey with Israel. Actually, He dwelt between the mercy seat and the cherubim (Ex. 25:22; I Sam. 4:4). In fact, it was actually the Holy Spirit, the third person of the Godhead we might say, who dwelt in the ark.

The ark contained the two tables of the Decalogue (the Ten Commandments), which constituted the documentary basis of God's redemptive covenant with Israel (Ex. 24:28-29). This redemption involved the life blood of the Redeemer (Ex. 24:8). The New Testament speaks appropriately of the death of the one who makes the will or *"testament"* (Heb. 9:16-18) and, hence, of the *"ark of His testament"* (Rev. 11:19).

The ark of the covenant represented in typology the new covenant, which was and is all in Christ and what He did for us at the cross.

Along with the two tablets of stone on which the Ten Commandments were inscribed, there was a pot of manna placed in the ark. The manna was a type of the Word of God.

As well, Aaron's rod, which budded (Num. 17:8-10), was also placed in the ark. The budded rod typified the death and resurrection of Christ.

Once every year the ark achieved its ultimate sacramental significance in the Day of Atonement service (Lev. 16:2).

After ensuring his personal safety through a protecting cloud of incense above it, Aaron would sprinkle the ark's cover, or mercy seat, seven times with blood: first with the blood of a bull, slain as a sin offering for himself, and then with that of a goat for the people so as to cleanse Israel *"from all your* (its) *sins before the* LORD*"* (Lev. 16:30).

In pictorial fashion, grace (the blood of the testament) thus became an intervening cover between the holiness of God (the glory cloud) and the verdict of divine justice upon the conduct of man.

The ark of God was never to be used as some type of magic talisman that would guarantee a victory for Israel. While the Lord commanded it to be used at times, it was only under His guidance and direction. In other words, we do not tell the Lord what to do; He tells us what to do.

## INSTRUCTIONS GIVEN BY THE HOLY SPIRIT TO JOSHUA

As we will see, every direction and every plan for crossing the Jordan was given by God. Neither Joshua nor any of the great officers of Israel contributed anything toward this which was to be done. It all came from the Lord. This should be a lesson for us.

Whatever it is, the Lord knows the way. Whatever we may think, we don't know the way. So, the only way that we're going to have victory in our lives is to do the thing exactly as the Lord has instructed us to do.

We will see in this example laid out before us that the cross of Christ is the means by which we receive everything. Of course, it is the Holy Spirit who makes it real to our lives, and we also know beyond the shadow of a doubt that the Lord Jesus is the source. Still, the cross is the means by which everything is done, in other words, the manner and the way that we receive all things from God.

## THE PRIESTS

The priests carried the ark on their shoulders, and the staves on each side of the ark were for that very purpose. They were types of Christ, who alone has the glory of God, represented by the ark. Jesus said to the prospective disciples, *"Follow Me."* He is still saying the same thing to millions of people. Regrettably, far too many are following other things.

Before the cross, men could not approach God, at least not directly, because the blood of bulls and goats could not take away sins (Heb. 10:4). Since the cross, we are invited to come boldly to the throne of grace, and to do so as often as we like (Heb. 4:16). As is here obvious, all the plans were God's plans and not at all of man. A perfect blueprint is laid out here for us. We should not fail to use it.

## THE PRIESTS, A TYPE OF CHRIST

Let us say it again: The ark was to be carried on the shoulders of priests, who were types of Christ. No one else could touch the ark under penalty of death.

Jesus said, *"I am the way, the truth, and the life: no man cometh unto the Father, but by me"* (John 14:6).

Let me put it this way:

- The only way to God is through Jesus Christ (John. 14:6).
- The only way to Jesus Christ is through the cross (Luke 9:23; 14:27).
- The only way to the cross is an abnegation of self (Luke 9:23).

## FOLLOW THE ARK

The Scripture plainly says, *"And go after it."* It also stated that there should be a space *"between ye and it, about two thousand cubits by measure."* This was a little over a half mile.

As stated, the people could not come near the ark with the penalty of death imposed upon anyone who did, other than the appointed priests. The reason was the following: The blood of bulls and goats could not take away sins (Heb. 10:4), so this means that the sin debt remained over the heads, so to speak, of every single person in Israel, and the world for that matter.

When Jesus went to the cross and shed His life's blood in order that we might be saved, He there atoned for all sin—past, present, and future—at least for all who will believe (John 1:29). In atoning for all sin, He lifted the sin debt. This means that the debt was totally and completely paid, and it was no longer owed by those who would accept Christ as Savior and Lord. Now that the cross of Christ is a fact, which means that all sin has been atoned, then this means that the sin debt is completely lifted, once again, for those who believe. This means that now believers can come unto the very throne of God, and do so at any time.

## THE THRONE OF GRACE

Concerning this, the Scripture says: *"Let us therefore come boldly unto the throne of grace* (presents the seat of divine power, and yet, the source of boundless grace), *that we may obtain mercy* (presents that which we want first), *and find grace to help in time of need* (refers to the goodness of God extended to all who come, and during any 'time of need'; all made possible by the cross)" (Heb. 4:16). – The Expositor's Study Bible

*"But now* (since the cross) *has He* (the Lord Jesus) *obtained a more excellent ministry* (the new covenant in Jesus' blood is superior and takes the place of the old covenant in animal blood), *by how much also He is the mediator of a better covenant* (proclaims the fact that Christ officiates between God and man according to the arrangements of the new covenant), *which was established upon better promises.* (This presents the new covenant, explicitly based on the cleansing and forgiveness of all sin, which the old covenant could not do)" (Heb. 8:6). – The Expositor's Study Bible

## SANCTIFICATION

*"And Joshua said unto the people, Sanctify yourselves: for tomorrow the LORD will do wonders among you. And Joshua spake unto the priests, saying, Take up the ark of the covenant, and pass*

*over before the people. And they took up the ark of the covenant,
and went before the people"* (Josh. 3:5-6).

Sanctification in Old Testament times was somewhat
different than now.

Due to the fact that the Holy Spirit could not reside in the
hearts and lives of believers as He can now, their sanctification
then consisted mostly of outward observances. They were to
bathe themselves and wash their clothing and, thereby, present
themselves before the Lord.

Since the cross, making it possible for the Holy Spirit to
come in and abide permanently within our hearts and lives,
sanctification takes on a brand-new process. The word *sanctify*
or *sanctification* actually means "to be set apart exclusively unto
the Lord." Now the Holy Spirit institutes and instigates the
sanctification process, with the requirement on our part being
that our faith rest supremely in Christ and the cross. This gives
the Holy Spirit latitude to work within our lives.

The problem with modern Christians is that we attempt
to sanctify ourselves, which we cannot do. As stated, this is a
work of the Holy Spirit, who alone can carry out the process.
As well, it is a process that, in effect, never ends, and is all made
possible by the cross (Rom. 8:1-11). In other words, there is
no graduating class in the sanctification process.

## WRONG DIRECTION

The truth is, most modern Christians have little or no idea
at all as to what the sanctification process actually is. Some have

tried to tie such to rules and regulations, to the type of clothing that's worn, looking at too much television, being too involved in sports, etc. The truth is that none of that stuff has anything to do whatsoever with sanctification, in other words, how that one is to be sanctified.

The moment that the believing sinner comes to Christ, without exception, such an individual is fully and totally sanctified. Paul said: *"And such were some of you* (before conversion)*: but you are washed* (refers to the blood of Jesus cleansing from all sin), *but you are sanctified* (one's position in Christ), *but you are justified* (declared not guilty) *in the name of the Lord Jesus* (refers to Christ and what He did at the cross in order that we might be saved), *and by the Spirit of our* God (proclaims the third person of the triune Godhead as the mechanic in this great work of grace)*"* (I Cor. 6:11). – The Expositor's Study Bible

We must understand that sanctification makes one clean while justification declares one clean. It's impossible for one to be declared clean before one is made clean. As well, the sanctification work that takes place at the moment of conversion is a perfect sanctification.

Now, that is our position in Christ, which never changes. We must understand that. It is not like mercury, which goes up and down, but it is standard. One might say that is our position in Christ, which is unchangeable.

However, Paul then said: *"And the very God of peace sanctify you wholly* (this is 'progressive sanctification,' which can only be brought about by the Holy Spirit, who does such as our

faith is firmly anchored in the cross, within which parameters the Spirit always works; the sanctification process involves the whole man); *and I pray God your whole spirit and soul and body* (proclaims the make-up of the whole man) *be preserved blameless unto the coming of our Lord Jesus Christ"* (I Thess. 5:23).
– The Expositor's Study Bible

So, at conversion we have positional sanctification, which, as stated, never changes, and in our everyday living for God, we have conditional sanctification, which changes almost by the day.

## THE WORK OF THE HOLY SPIRIT

The moment the believing sinner comes to Christ, the Holy Spirit sets about in the heart and life of such a person to bring his condition up to his position. It's a process that really never ends and will continue until the trump sounds or the Lord calls the believer home. This conditional work is where most believers have their problems.

We try to sanctify ourselves, and no matter how zealous we might be and no matter how sincere we might be, it simply cannot be done. So, how can it be done? The believer is to place his or her faith exclusively in Christ and the cross, and maintain it exclusively in Christ and the cross. Then the Holy Spirit can work within his life and bring about that which He desires. This is the only way it can be done (Rom. 8:1-11).

It is the cross that gives the Holy Spirit the legal right to do all that He does. Before the cross, due to the fact that the blood of bulls and goats could not take away sins, this meant that the sin debt was still there, even in the heart and life of the most ardent believer. Consequently, this stopped the Holy Spirit from coming into the heart and life of the believer. While He could come into the heart of some, such as prophets, etc., to enable them to carry out their tasks, when those tasks were completed, He left out. However, when Jesus died on the cross, He atoned for all sin—past, present, and future. This means that upon simple faith in Christ, the Holy Spirit comes into the heart and life of the believing sinner, there to abide permanently.

John said when quoting the words of our Lord: *"And I will pray the Father, and he shall give you another comforter* ('Parakletos,' which means 'one called to the side of another to help'), *that he may abide with you forever; Even the Spirit of truth; whom the world cannot receive, because it seeth him not, neither knoweth him: but ye know him; for he dwelleth with you, and shall be in you"* (John. 14:16-17).

So, the sanctification process for the believer is to place his faith exclusively in Christ and what He did for us at the cross, and maintain it there. With that being done, the Holy Spirit can begin His work within our lives, which will never end. That means that the believer is always in the sanctification process. While we have a position of sanctification, which cannot be changed, as it regards our condition, the Holy Spirit is constantly working on us and in us to carry out the work that is desired. In other words, He wants to rid us of all sin. No, while the Bible does not teach sinless perfection, it most definitely does teach that sin is not to have dominion over us (Rom. 6:14).

So, as we've already stated, the sanctification process was altogether different in Old Testament times, for the simple reason that the Holy Spirit was greatly limited then as to what He could do due to the weakness of animal blood. Now, the blood of our Lord Jesus Christ has been applied to our hearts and lives, and to be sure, it cleanses from all sin (I John 1:7).

## SELF AND SANCTIFICATION

All so-called sanctification by self, in other words, by rules and regulations, always and without fail leads to self-righteousness. Sanctification by the Holy Spirit, which is by the means of the cross, leads to humility. Yet the modern church, if it looks at sanctification at all, attempts to do so by the means of self. It cannot be done that way.

I read the other day that America's pastime once was baseball. It is now self improvement. Let it be understood that it is completely impossible for a person to sanctify himself or herself by the means of self. It cannot be done. But I'm afraid the modern church has borrowed the ways of the world, and the end result will be for the Christian the same that it is for the unredeemed—a wasted effort. And yet, there's something in us that delights in hearing how wonderful we are, how great we are, how we have a champion living inside of us, and how we can change ourselves.

Please understand the following: There is no such thing as moral evolution. In other words, we are not steadily and gradually getting better and better, but outside of Christ, we are getting worse and worse. Let me say it again: There is no such thing as moral evolution. However, there is something in mankind, even believers, that desires to do that which is of ourselves, but such is impossible. God's way is the cross of Christ. He has no other way because no other way is needed. He doesn't require much of us, but He does require one thing—that our faith be exclusively in Christ and the cross (Rom. 6:1-14; I Cor. 1:17-18, 23; 2:2; Gal. 6:14; Col. 2:10-15). The cross is His way and, in fact, has always been His way and will ever be His way.

## YOU SHALL STAND STILL IN JORDAN

*"And the L*ORD *said unto Joshua, This day will I begin to magnify thee in the sight of all Israel, that they may know that, as I was with Moses, so I will be with thee. And you shall command the priests that bear the ark of the covenant, saying, When ye are come to the brink of the water of Jordan, ye shall stand still in Jordan"* (Josh. 3:7-8).

While deliverance from Egypt can definitely be described as a type of the salvation experience, it also can be typed as deliverance from the dominion of the sin nature (Rom. 6:14).

In fact, while in Egypt, the Lord referred to the Israelites as *"My people"* (Ex. 3:7). They were saved, not by being delivered out of Egypt, but by trusting in the Abrahamic covenant, which, in effect, was justification by faith (Gen. 15:6). That deliverance was effected, even as it is effected presently, by faith in what the slain lamb represented, which was the coming Redeemer (Ex. 12:13).

In the wilderness, Israel ceased to have faith in the slain lamb and, thereby, wandered aimlessly for some thirty-eight years, with an entire generation dying in that wasteland. Regrettably and sadly, millions of modern Christians follow suit. They take their faith away from the slain lamb and place it in something else. Such a direction always guarantees failure.

As we have already stated, crossing the Jordan is a type of the baptism with the Holy Spirit, for it is impossible to claim the promises of God without the leading, guidance, and power of the Spirit, who always works within the framework of Christ and the cross (Rom. 8:2).

## FACING PROBLEMS ACCORDING TO THE DIRECTIONS OF THE HOLY SPIRIT

The river Jordan presented a formidable obstacle to Israel as it regarded their entering the promised land, especially considering that it was now at flood tide. As stated, normally the Jordan River is only about fifty to one hundred feet wide; however, in those years, due to not drawing water out of the river for irrigation as is presently done, the river would flood in the spring. According to scholars, it was probably about a mile and a half wide at this time and about forty feet deep.

The Holy Spirit, without a doubt, chose the most inopportune time of the year for the crossing to be made. In fact, without a miracle, it was virtually impossible for some three million Israelites, along with all of their herds, to get across this obstacle.

Even if they had built a small fleet of boats, it would have taken upwards of a year to get everyone across this body of water.

So, in effect, there was nothing physically that could be done to speed up the process. It was either God or nothing!

The directions were that the priests bearing the ark of the covenant were to come *"to the brink of the water of Jordan,"* referring to the edge of the river. They were to then *"stand still in Jordan."*

## OBSTACLES

Every advancement made by the child of God is always met by a formidable obstacle presented by Satan. To be sure, the Lord allows Satan certain latitude in order to teach believers faith and trust. We have to learn and understand that there is nothing God cannot do. Whatever obstacles that Satan throws in our path, no matter what they might be, the Lord can easily help us around them, over them, through them, etc. He is not limited unless we limit Him by unbelief.

As well, as here typified, we do not overcome problems by trying to ignore them or by trying to confess that they do not exist. It would have been useless for Joshua and the children of Israel to confess that the Jordan River wasn't there. How silly can we be? Problems, obstacles, hindrances, and difficulties cannot be confessed away; they must be met head-on, but we must remember how they are to be met.

The Lord didn't tell the officers—the mighty men of Israel—to go stand on the edge of Jordan, and neither did the Lord tell any of the children of Israel to perform this task. It was instructed that the priests, who were bearing the ark of the covenant, were themselves to go to the brink of Jordan and there stand in that body of water. We should learn a lesson from this.

## LISTEN TO PAUL

All too often we attempt to do things that we cannot do. Inasmuch as the priests who were bearing the ark were types of Christ, and the ark itself was a type of the throne of God, it was Christ alone who could perform the task, and, in effect, it was the Holy Spirit.

Concerning the living of this Christian life, the great apostle said (which I lift directly from The Expositor's Study Bible):

*I am crucified with Christ* (as the foundation of all victory; Paul here takes us back to Romans 6:3-5): *nevertheless I live* (have new life); *yet not I* (not by my own strength and ability), *but Christ lives in me* (by virtue of me dying with Him on the cross and being raised with Him in newness of life): *and the life which I now live in the flesh* (my daily walk before God) *I live by the faith of the Son of God* (the cross is ever the object of my faith), *who loved me, and gave Himself for me* (which is the only way that I could be saved). *I do not frustrate the grace of God* (if we make anything other than the cross of Christ the object of our faith, we frustrate the grace of God, which means we stop its action, and the Holy Spirit is greatly hindered in trying to help us): *for if righteousness come by the law* (any type of law), *then Christ is dead in vain.*

(If I can successfully live for the Lord by any means other than faith in Christ and the cross, then the death of Christ was a waste) (Gal. 2:20-21).

In a nutshell, so to speak, we face obstacles, ever how large they might be, by making certain that our faith is anchored squarely in Christ and the cross. This is the same thing as one's faith being anchored squarely in the Word, for they are all synonymous. This then allows the Holy Spirit the proper latitude within our lives. He can bring about whatever it is that we need (Rom. 6:1-14; 8:1-11).

The idea is to go toward your problem instead of running from it, but at the same time, make certain that it is Christ who leads the charge. Our faith in His cross guarantees that (I Cor. 1:17-18, 23; 2:2; Galatians 5).

## COME HERE AND HEAR THE WORDS
## OF THE LORD YOUR GOD

*"And Joshua said unto the children of Israel, Come hither and hear the words of the LORD your God. And Joshua said, Hereby ye shall know that the living God is among you, and that he will without fail drive out from before you the Canaanites, and the Hittites, and the Hivites, and the Perizzites, and the Girgashites, and the Amorites, and the Jebusites"* (Josh. 3:9-10).

Joshua would now address Israel, and he told them at the beginning, *"Come hither and hear the words of the LORD your God."* In other words, what Israel would hear would not be the mere words of Joshua, as weighty as they may have been, but rather *"the words of the* LORD.*"*

While the Bible is silent concerning this, it is positive that the Lord had told Joshua exactly what He wanted him to do. In other words, Joshua did not form these plans. Looking at that swollen river approximately a mile and a half wide and some forty feet deep, there was nothing that man could do. So, the Lord had informed Joshua what was going to be done, and to be sure, it would be a miracle of unprecedented proportions. The only miracle that was greater was the opening of the Red Sea, but this great miracle was not very far behind. In other words, everything that Joshua was here saying were *"the words of the* LORD *your God."*

What held true then holds true now, and perfectly so. Too many are running over the landscape, saying, "God told me," when the Lord hasn't told them anything. If it's the Lord, what He says will always and without fail come to pass.

## THE LIVING GOD AND THE ENEMIES OF ISRAEL

The Lord told Joshua to tell the people that there, in fact, were enemies in the promised land. He even named the tribes—some seven in totality.

The Lord could have done any number of things to rid the land of these enemies of the people of God; however, as stated, He allowed them to remain in order that Israel might learn faith and trust.

He said that *"without fail,"* He would drive out these enemies; however, as we shall see, that depended on obedience to the word of God. It is always obedience! We are given the word, and we are to obey that word, whatever it might be.

To be sure, the Lord still speaks to His people today. He is the same with us as He was with Joshua. If the believer will earnestly seek the face of the Lord as it regards leading and guidance, to be sure, the Lord will answer that prayer and will give the leading and the guidance. Until He does, stay where you are.

## THE LORD OF ALL THE EARTH

Israel was the only monotheistic nation on the face of the earth. This meant that they worshipped one God—Jehovah. The other nations of the world were polytheistic, which means they worshipped many gods, actually, demon spirits. However, Joshua 3:11 of this passage plainly tells us that Jehovah is *"the Lord of all the earth,"* and not these heathenistic gods, which, in effect, were no gods at all!

At this present time, there are about two billion people on the earth who go under the guise of Christian. There are about one billion Protestants and about one billion Catholics. Of course, as to how many people of this number are truly saved, only the Lord would know, but one thing is certain: that number is probably infinitesimally small.

There are about 1.3 billion Muslims in the world and about one half billion Buddhists and Shintoists. The balance of the world is made up of atheists and whatever. So the situation now is not so very much different than it was 3,500 years ago at the time of Joshua. However, irrespective of the religious beliefs of these false religions, Jesus Christ is still the Lord of all the earth. One day soon He will reign personally from Jerusalem. This reign will commence almost immediately after the second coming (Rev. 19).

*Blessed Lord in Thee is refuge,*
*Safety for my trembling soul,*
*Power to lift my head when drooping*
*'Midst the angry billows' roll.*
*I will trust Thee, I will trust Thee;*
*All my life Thou shall control.*

*In the past, too, unbelieving,*
*'Midst the tempest I have been,*
*And my heart has slowly trusted*
*What my eyes have never seen.*
*Blessed Jesus, blessed Jesus,*
*Teach me on Thy arm to lean.*

*Oh, for trust, that brings the triumph,*
*When defeat seems strangely near;*
*Oh, for faith, that changes fighting*
*Into victory's ringing cheer:*
*Faith triumphant, faith triumphant,*
*Knowing not defeat nor fear.*

# RAHAB

## AND OTHER

# MIRACLES

CHAPTER 4

THE MIRACLE

# THE MIRACLE

## THE GOVERNMENT OF GOD

Now Joshua is told by the Lord to *"take you twelve men out of the tribes of Israel, out of every tribe a man"* (Josh. 3:12).

We aren't given any information here as to what these men were to do; however, Joshua 4:1 does shed some light on the subject.

As we have stated, the number twelve in the Bible stands for the government of God. However, understand that it is the government of God and not the government of man. There were twelve tribes of Israel and twelve apostles. As we have also stated, the government of God is the Word of God.

One of the greatest problems in the church, and a problem that seems to have always existed, is that religious man attempts to replace the government of God with his own government, whatever that might be. Many religious denominations begin in the right way by looking solely to the Word of God. They are then blessed somewhat and begin to intrude upon the government of the Lord by attempting to replace it with their own government. It always brings tragedy.

One particular time I was speaking to a religious leader when he stated something that was obviously unscriptural. I kindly made mention of this to him, and his answer was very revealing. He did not deny that what he said was unscriptural, but rather, he stated, "But that is our tradition." In other words, "It doesn't really matter about the situation being unscriptural; it's just what we want to do." Such a direction always spells disaster.

The Word of God must be the criterion for all things. We must not veer from the Word, deviate from the Word, add to the Word, or take from the Word. Jesus said, *"Man shall not live by bread alone, but by every word that proceeds out of the mouth of God"* (Matt. 4:4).

Tragically, we have a tendency to not obey the admonition of our Lord, but rather to substitute something to take its place. The government of God must never be abrogated, weakened, or substituted in any way.

## THE PROMISE OF THE LORD

According to Joshua 3:13, the children of Israel now knew how they were going to cross the Jordan. The Lord was going to perform a miracle, in fact, a miracle of unprecedented proportions.

The actual terminology in the Hebrew is, *"And they shall stand, one heap,"* referring to the waters of the Jordan River.

Some claim that it was an earthquake that caused this. Whatever it was that the Lord used to bring about this tremendous miracle really doesn't matter. The idea is that it was not happenchance or happenstance, but rather a miracle generated totally by the Lord. This was what the Lord said that He would do, and as we shall see, it is most definitely what He did do.

> *And it came to pass, when the people removed from their tents, to pass over Jordan, and the priests bearing the ark of the covenant before the people; And as they that bare the ark were come unto Jordan, and the feet of the priests that bare the ark were dipped in the brim of the water, (for Jordan overfloweth all his banks all the time of harvest,) That the waters which came down from above stood and rose up upon an heap very far from the city Adam, that is beside Zaretan: and those that came down toward the sea of the plain, even the salt sea, failed, and were cut off: and the people passed over right against Jericho. And the priests that bare the ark of the covenant of the LORD stood firm on dry ground in the midst of Jordan, and all the Israelites passed over on dry ground, until all the people were passed clean over Jordan* (Josh. 3:14-17).

## THE POWER OF GOD

No doubt, due to the fact of Jordan being flooded and now about a mile and a half wide, the people of Jericho felt somewhat safe, with them thinking that Israel could not cross the swollen river. They reckoned without the power of God.

The opening of the Jordan can be construed as none other than one of the greatest miracles ever performed by the Lord.

Furthermore, the Lord had them to cross opposite Jericho, with the inhabitants of that city, no doubt, observing this spectacle.

Many people think of Jordan as described here as a type of death, with Canaan as a type of heaven. However, while Jordan is a type of death, it is rather a type of the death of the flesh, with Canaan being a type of our possession of the promises of God by the power of the Holy Spirit. In other words, the promised land is a type of the inheritance of the child of God, but which can be obtained only by the power of the Holy Spirit.

## THE GREAT MIRACLE

The idea of the opening of the Jordan seems to have been that the Lord effected the opening some fifteen or twenty miles above where Israel was camped, with a dry riverbed running all the way to the Dead Sea, into which the Jordan normally emptied. Considering that nearly three million people had to cross, plus all of their herds (ever how many there were), the actual crossing had to be several miles wide, which it, no doubt, was. I wonder what the thoughts of the inhabitants of Jericho actually were as they observed this miraculous happening—watching hundreds of thousands of the children of Israel cross the dry riverbed. I suspect that Rahab and her family were watching intently as well. I'm sure that every moment that they watched, Rahab was remembering the promise that the two spies had made to her: she and her family would be spared.

Let it be understood that the God of miracles of yesterday is still the God of miracles today. Far too many claim the days of miracles are over; however, there is nothing in the Word of God that substantiates such a claim. In fact, the Lord changes not.

## TWELVE MEN

> *And it came to pass, when all the people were clean passed over Jordan, that the* LORD *spake unto Joshua, saying, Take you twelve men out of the people, out of every tribe a man, And command ye them, saying, Take you hence out of the midst of Jordan, out of the place where the priests' feet stood firm, twelve stones, and you shall carry them over with you, and leave them in the lodging place, where ye shall lodge this night. Then Joshua called the twelve men, whom he had prepared of the children of Israel, out of every tribe a man: And Joshua said unto them, Pass over before the ark of the* LORD *your God into the midst of Jordan, and take ye up every man of you a stone upon his shoulder, according unto the number of the tribes of the children of Israel (Josh. 4:1-5).*

*"Take you twelve men out of the people."* As is obvious, this was a man for each tribe. As previously stated, the number twelve represents government and, in reality, God's government. As well, it meant that every single person who passed across enjoyed the same type of salvation. None were saved more than others; likewise, the born-again experience for the vilest libertine is the same as the salvation experience for the good moral man. Both are horribly lost, and both must have a glorious salvation; consequently, salvation is the same for both.

These twelve men, one from each tribe, were to take a stone each to Gilgal and set them up as a memorial. Incidentally, the name *Gilgal* means "rolled away." Where Israel was encamped and what Israel was instructed by the Lord to do, in effect, stated, "The wilderness experience of doubt and death is all rolled away. It is no more held against us. It is gone, forever gone!"

## A SIGN

> *That this may be a sign among you, that when your children ask their fathers in time to come, saying, What mean ye by these stones? Then ye shall answer them, That the waters of Jordan were cut off before the ark of the covenant of the LORD; when it passed over Jordan, the waters of Jordan were cut off: and these stones shall be for a memorial unto the children of Israel forever. And the children of Israel did so as Joshua commanded, and took up twelve stones out of the midst of Jordan, as the LORD spake unto Joshua, according to the number of the tribes of the children of Israel, and carried them over with them unto the place where they lodged, and laid them down there (Josh. 4:6-8).*

## THE TESTIMONY

In the years to come, even the centuries to come, when the children would ask their fathers what the stones meant, the testimony was to be the same. They were to tell the children how the Lord delivered them. As well, the testimony of the salvation experience must ever be the same. As it was for the fathers, it is so for the children. The message must not change.

The stones represent the great power of God in delivering Israel from the wilderness as well as from Egypt. The great rock, the Lord Jesus Christ, represents our salvation and must be told the same to the children as to the fathers. God help us when the children ask what this means that we will instantly tell them the miraculous story: saved by grace.

## THE MEMORIAL

Joshua 4:7 says, *"Shall be for a memorial."* What is our memorial today? Too often it is the rank message of modernism, which denies the mighty power of God, the false cults that substitute another ark, or, sadly, the church that preaches another gospel, which is the opposite of the message—Jesus Christ and Him crucified (I Cor. 1:23).

## THE MESSAGE OF THE CROSS

I'm afraid that now when the children ask what the church presently believes, the answer given them is no longer what it was yesteryear. The message in the early church was Jesus Christ and Him crucified (Rom. 6:1-14; I Cor. 1:17-18, 21, 23; 2:2; Gal. 2:20-21; 5; 6:14; Col. 2:14-15).

Regrettably, most modern churches have a program, in fact, a well-oiled program, but they have no message. Let it ever be understood that the reason for the church, the purpose for the church, and the cause for the church is the message. As stated, the modern church has no message; it has only a program!

Let me hurriedly say the following: If it's not the message of the cross, whatever else it claims to be, it is no message at all, at least that will save people.

## THE WILDERNESS STONES

> And Joshua set up twelve stones in the midst of Jordan, in the place where the feet of the priests which bare the ark of the covenant stood: and they are there unto this day. For the priests which bare the ark stood in the midst of Jordan, until everything was finished that the LORD commanded Joshua to speak unto the people, according to all that Moses commanded Joshua: and the people hasted and passed over. And it came to pass, when all the people were clean passed over, that the ark of the LORD passed over, and the priests, in the presence of the people. And the children of Reuben, and the children of Gad, and half the tribe of Manasseh, passed over armed before the children of Israel, as Moses spake unto them: About forty thousand prepared for war passed over before the LORD unto battle, to the plains of Jericho. On that day the LORD magnified Joshua in the sight of all Israel; and they feared him, as they feared Moses, all the days of his life (Josh. 4:9-14).

## TWO MEMORIALS

We find in Joshua 4 that there are two distinct memorials set up, with both consisting of twelve stones each.

Four facts are stated about these stones. They were *taken,* they were *carried,* they were *laid down,* and they were *set up.* The origin of the stones was the deep bed of Jordan. Their purpose was to testify that Israel owed her entrance into the goodly land only and wholly to divine grace and power.

In the baptism into Christ, the believer dies to his old life and rises into a new life. We are reminded that as to our moral origin, we were buried beneath the waters of the wrath of God; that as to our present position, we are now set up upon resurrection ground; and it is our duty to testify daily to the glory of Christ, the one and only Savior. The Lord Jesus Christ said to the Pharisees that if the children were silent, the very stones would cry out (Luke 19:40). These stones set up at Gilgal cried out day and night (Rom. 6:1-5).

The first memorial could, no doubt, be referred to as Jordan stones, but these spoken of in Joshua 4:9 must be referred to as wilderness stones. These twelve stones buried on the bottom of the Jordan River, where the feet of the priests had stood, signified the death and burial of Israel's forty years of unbelief and sinning in the wilderness.

## FOREVER COVERED

The Lord was saying to Israel that that time was over, buried, out of sight, and forgotten, which is typical of all of our sins of the past, that is, if we have properly trusted Christ (I John 1:9). Unfortunately, far too many modern Christians seem to take delight in diving down to the bottom of Jordan, spiritually speaking, and retrieving these stones and bringing them to the surface. Therefore, they are constantly reminding people of such-and-such sin. I hope we can see the terrible insult to Christ that such a thing is and, in fact, that such action is sinful and wicked. Sins forgiven are to never be held over someone's head.

What a scene this must have been! The majestic ark of the covenant was held on the shoulders of the priests, and all were in the middle of Jordan, with the waters held up by the mighty power of God so that the people could walk across on dry ground, flood or not! Joshua was a type of Christ, who actually carried the Hebrew name *Joshua,* which means "Savior." The Greek derivative is *Jesus.*

## THE FEET OF THE PRIESTS WHICH BORE
## THE ARK OF THE COVENANT STOOD

Joshua 4:9 says, *"And Joshua set up twelve stones in the midst of Jordan."* These twelve stones were totally different from the twelve that they had taken out of Jordan. As stated, these could be called wilderness stones. They represent the terrible failure, sin, and defeat of the wilderness. In effect, Joshua was saying, "In the sea of God's forgetfulness."

The Lord was telling Israel that the wilderness is forgotten, the failures are buried, and they will be covered by the Jordan, not to be remembered anymore.

They were to be placed *"where the feet of the priests which bare the ark of the covenant stood."* Every sin of the past is washed by the precious blood of Jesus Christ. They are buried forever, not to be remembered against us anymore.

It says, *"And they are there unto this day."* Those stones representing the horrible wilderness failure were to be covered by the waters of God's grace. They were not to be seen anymore, and neither were they to be remembered anymore. In the eyes of God, they no longer existed.

As we have previously stated, sadly, too many Christians seem to delight in diving into the murky waters of life's Jordan and groping around on the bed of the sea of God's forgetfulness. Then, when they find a stone, whether the correct one or not, they delight in bringing it to the surface and calling it to the attention of all concerned.

How the anger of God would have burned red hot if the Israelites had attempted to retrieve these buried wilderness stones! How God's anger must burn red hot today when Christians attempt to retrieve, to remember, or to rehash that which God has forgiven, cleansed, and forgotten. Why should we remember what He has forgotten?

## FORGETTING THOSE THINGS WHICH ARE BEHIND

Likewise, when Satan comes to us and attempts to bring his condemnation of past failures, we must do as Paul said, *"Forgetting those things which are behind"* (Phil. 3:13). Hallelujah!

What a sight this must have been. Nearly three million people flooding across the dry bed of Jordan, with the priests dressed in their royal garments holding the ark of the covenant on their shoulders. What must the inhabitants of Jericho have thought? No doubt, stark fear filled their hearts, as well it should!

Truly,

*Jesus is the one, yes He's the only one.*

*Let Him have His way, until the day is done,*

*When He speaks you know,*

*The dark clouds will have to go,*

*Just because He loves you so.*

## THE DIVINE WAY

And the LORD spake unto Joshua, saying; Command the priests that bear the ark of the testimony, that they come up out of Jordan. Joshua therefore commanded the priests, saying, Come ye up out of Jordan. And it came to pass, when the priests that bare the ark of the covenant of the LORD were come up out of the midst of Jordan, and the soles of the priests' feet were lifted up unto the dry land, that the waters of Jordan returned unto their place, and flowed over all his banks, as they did before (Josh. 4:15-18).

This is the way of the Lord: He calls men and women, and then He speaks to them, giving leading and guidance. Unfortunately, most of the church has long since ceased to hear from the Lord, that is, if they ever heard from Him. They are, thereby, led by men, and the results are obvious.

Williams says, "There was but one way into Canaan and that the divine way made by the ark of the covenant."[1]

There is but one way to heaven, and Jesus said, *"I am the way"* (John 14:6). The ark typified Him—its precious wood, His humanity; its gold, His deity; its blood-sprinkled cover, His atonement. As the ark descended into the depths of Jordan and rolled back its waters, so Christ descended into the deep waters of the wrath of God and opened the one way into everlasting life.

## THE ARK OF THE COVENANT

If it is to be noticed, Joshua 4:16 proclaims the ark of the covenant being referred to as the *"ark of the testimony."* The word *testimony* in the Hebrew means "witness," so it could be called the "ark of the witness."

This means that the ark of the covenant was a witness given by God of His promises as it regarded the coming Redeemer. The ark witnessed to that promise—that coming event!

When Israel no longer cared, and I'm referring to caring about the coming Redeemer, the ark of the covenant was lost, which took place about a thousand years into the future. Some say that Jeremiah hid it in a cave, and he did so immediately before the Babylonian invasion. One thing is known: When the Babylonians broke into the Holy of Holies at the temple, there was no ark of the covenant. What actually happened to it, we aren't told.

## THE MIRACLE

Joshua 4:18 says that at the moment the priest walked out of the bed of Jordan to yonder bank, *"the waters of Jordan returned* unto their place, and flowed over all his banks, as they did before." Some claim that this was merely an earthquake that took place and had nothing to do with the miracle-working power of God. In other words, they are claiming a natural phenomenon. Nothing could be further from the truth!

As to exactly how the Lord did this thing, we aren't told. However, we do know that whatever was done was supernatural, which is proven by the fact that the moment the priests left the riverbed, the waters returned. It would be impossible to calculate an earthquake and its effects to that degree. No, this was the miracle-working power of God that opened that river, even though it was at flood tide. Let all know and understand that God is still in the miracle-working business.

## GILGAL

> And the people came up out of Jordan on the tenth day of the first month, and encamped in Gilgal, in the east border of Jericho. And those twelve stones, which they took out of Jordan, did Joshua pitch in Gilgal. And he spoke unto the children of Israel, saying, When your children shall ask their fathers in time to come, saying, What mean these stones? Then ye shall let your children know, saying, Israel came over this Jordan on dry land. For the LORD your God dried up the waters of Jordan from before you, until ye were passed over, as the LORD your God did to the Red sea, which He dried up from before us, until we were gone over: That all the people of the earth might know the hand of the LORD, that it is mighty: that ye might fear the LORD your God forever (Josh. 4:19-24).

As previously stated, the name *Gilgal* means "rolled away." Their encampment in this place typified that the sins, doubt, and unbelief of the wilderness had rolled away.

Gilgal was an appropriate place for these twelve memorial stones to be set up. In a sense, it was a new beginning for Israel. With faith in Christ, any individual can have a new beginning.

The miracles of the past that the Lord has given us to be related again and again, in essence, are lived again and again. While we cannot live off past miracles, they do give us faith for the present time and the future, which they are meant to do.

Of the nearly three million people who left Egypt some forty years before, other than those under twenty years of age, only two of them would actually go into the promised land: Joshua and Caleb. Doubt and unbelief killed the others, while faith brought Joshua and Caleb through.

## THE SINS ARE ROLLED AWAY

*"The tenth day of the first month,"* corresponds somewhat with our modern April. This was the time of the barley harvest—the time of the Passover.

Presently, Jericho is about five miles due west of the Jordan River. Considering that this river was at flood tide, approximately a mile and a half wide from the banks of the river, then to Jericho was about three and a half miles. So, the area referred to as Gilgal was probably about two miles from Jericho, or possibly as little as a mile and a half. It is believed that the army of Jericho was powerful, and yet, they made no attempt to come against Israel.

## THE REASON?

The reason was the manner and the way that Israel crossed the Jordan. With the river being at flood tide and approximately a mile and a half wide and some forty feet deep, quite possibly, the inhabitants of Jericho felt somewhat secure. And yet, there was the nagging truth of what had transpired some forty years before when the Red Sea miraculously opened.

I personally think that the inhabitants of Jericho hardly knew what to do. Could they come out and fight people who had just seen and witnessed such a miracle, and for whom this miracle had been tendered? Therefore, they did what Joshua 6:1 proclaims, *"Jericho was straitly shut up because of the children of Israel: none went out, and none came in."*

## THE PAST

I think that one could say without fear of contradiction that most everything that Israel now did was a type of redemption and the moving and operation of the Holy Spirit.

As stated, Gilgal was an appropriate place for them to camp. It spoke of a new beginning, especially considering that the very name *Gilgal* meant "rolled away." Every person in the world, in some way, has a past. Of course, with some, that past is extremely negative, and with others, it is less so; nevertheless, a past of some sort is present with all. Suffice to say that most would like to have certain parts of their past erased, which, of course, is impossible in the natural. But yet, it can be done, just as this illustration of

Gilgal gives to us. It can be done in Christ. As someone has well said, "The child of God has no past, while Satan has no future."

What a statement!

The Lord was telling Israel when they encamped at Gilgal that the past was done away with. The terrible wilderness experience that lasted for some forty years, which saw such heartache, death, and dying, was now gone and erased. In fact, that was typified by the twelve stones that were placed in the darkened depths of Jordan.

## A NEW BEGINNING

Israel had a new beginning, and any believer can have a new beginning, irrespective of what the past has been, if they will only look to Christ. Look to Christ! Look to Christ and what He did for us at the cross! Calvary erased the past, and did so totally and completely. As well, it promised and guaranteed a brand-new future. Nothing in the world can touch that; nothing in the world can equal that; and nothing in the world can even remotely approach that.

There is one more thing that needs to be said about the Lord. Some may read these words and say, "Brother Swaggart, you don't understand. I've tried my best in the Lord to start over again and again, and I keep failing."

As bad as that is, let it ever be understood that God has no limitation on the times that one can begin again. As long as we meet His condition, which is to simply confess our failure to Him, He will always be *"faithful and just to forgive us our sins, and to cleanse us from all unrighteousness"* (I John 1:9).

## THE MEMORIAL

As is obvious here, the Lord wanted future generations to never forget the great miracle that had been performed on this tenth day of April, which was the first month of Israel's year. The exciting, supernatural, and miraculous story must be told again and again! So should every miracle given in the Word of God, as well as those that happened to us personally, be told over and over.

They should be told, *"That all the people of the earth might know the hand of the LORD, that it is mighty: that you might fear the LORD your God forever."*

Regrettably and sadly, this has not been done and is not now being done, at least to the degree that it should; however, there is coming a day that the entirety of the earth will *"know the hand of the LORD."* I speak of the coming kingdom age when Jesus will rule and reign in person from Jerusalem. Then and only then will things be as they ought to be. Now the world points to the very opposite—global warming or freezing temperatures—in other words, coming catastrophes for this world. To be sure, were it left in the hands of man, it would be a catastrophe; however, Jesus Christ, its creator, is coming back, and as the song says, "What a day that will be!"

## CIRCUMCISION

*And it came to pass, when all the kings of the Amorites, which were on the side of Jordan westward, and all the kings of the*

*Canaanites, which were by the sea, heard that the* LORD *had dried up the waters of Jordan from before the children of Israel, until we were passed over, that their heart melted, neither was there spirit in them anymore, because of the children of Israel. At that time the* LORD *said unto Joshua, Make thee sharp knives, and circumcise again the children of Israel the second time. And Joshua made him sharp knives, and circumcised the children of Israel at the hill of the foreskins. And this is the cause why Joshua did circumcise: All the people who came out of Egypt who were males, even all the men of war, died in the wilderness by the way, after they came out of Egypt. Now all the people who came out were circumcised: but all the people who were born in the wilderness by the way as they came forth out of Egypt, them they had not circumcised* (Josh. 5:1-5).

Even though the hearts of the kings of the Amorites melted with fear before Israel, still, they would oppose Israel. No matter what, Satan will oppose the child of God, but victory is assured if God's way is followed, even as did Joshua.

Israel was about to smite the seven nations of Canaan with the sword of the Lord. Williams says, "But before they were fitted to use the sword on others, they must themselves feel its sharpness and 'die beneath its stroke.' This was illustrated in circumcision, which, in essence, is a type of the cross. "Separation was made, and blood was shed. We as believers are to be separated from the world, and this can only be done by looking to Christ and the cross, which latter the blood symbolizes."[2]

## MAN'S PERSONAL GOODNESS MUST BE SLAIN

Those who are fitted to use the sword of the Spirit, which is the Word of God, have themselves experienced the death-stroke that it gives to nature—that is, to the natural man. Only they have been given the wisdom and the goodness.

It is most bitter to man to learn that all of his goodness must be slain with the sword of the Lord just as much as all of his badness. However, to the true believer, this is most sweet, for it brings him into a resurrection life, and the power of that life takes all strength from Satan. Man as man, let him be ever so religious, has no strength against Satan. Jericho's walls never fall before him.

So circumcision was a symbol of Christ and the cross and the price that He would there pay in order to deliver fallen humanity. In the face of the enemy, Joshua circumcised all the men of war, which rendered the entirety of the male population helpless. However, their weakness would be their strength (II Cor. 12:9-10).

The reproach of Egypt was dual. So long as Israel wandered in the wilderness, Egypt reproached them with the taunt that Jehovah could not bring them into the promised land. Further, all of Egypt that attaches to a servant of God is a reproach to Him. That double reproach was rolled away at Gilgal.

## SATAN'S FORTRESSES

This is a powerful portrayal of what God demands in order that we have victory. His demands will be totally opposite of that which the world demands.

Jericho was a fortress. It barred Israel's entrance into the promised land. Likewise, Satan has placed many fortresses at the entrance of the promises that God has made for us. He desires to keep us from inheriting that which God has promised us. As Jericho's conquest was impossible to Israel, at least as far as the flesh was concerned, likewise, our victory respecting the great fortresses that Satan has reared is impossible for us in the flesh as well. Let us see what the Lord required of Israel that day, and what He requires of us today.

## SATAN TREMBLES IN THE FACE OF THE NAME OF JESUS

The Scripture said, *"That their heart melted, neither was there spirit in them anymore, because of the children of Israel."*

Joshua 5:1 of this narrative speaks of all the kings with their mighty fortresses who would oppose Israel. Yet, their hearts melted. Satan would attempt to make us believe that our opposition is so formidable that it is hopeless, especially considering the times (possibly so) that we tried and failed. However, in spiritual reality, the opposite is true.

The Spirit of God had so worked on these enemies of Israel that they literally trembled in fear of the people of God. In spiritual reality, Satan trembles in fear at the power of God manifest in us. He doesn't want us to know it. He tries to hide it from us. He tries to make us believe that our opposition is so strong that we cannot hope to overcome. That is one of his chief tactics. In reality, he is already defeated, and his heart is trembling in fear. In fact, he was defeated at Calvary's cross, and he was defeated in totality (Col. 2:14-15).

We should understand this, and we should know this. We should shout the praises of God constantly. We should understand that instead of fear plaguing us, it is fear that plagues the enemy— *"their heart melted."* All of us want these great victories, and in this narrative, we are given God's blueprint for victory:

- Jesus Christ is the source of all blessings we receive from God.
- The cross of Christ is the means by which all of these wonderful things are made available to us.
- All of this means that the cross of Christ must ever be the object of our faith. This is critically important.
- With Jesus as the source, the cross as the means, and the cross of Christ the object of our faith, then the Holy Spirit, who works exclusively within the parameters of the finished work of Christ, will work mightily on our behalf. However, it's only within the parameters of the cross of Christ that He works. That's the reason it is imperative that the cross of Christ ever be the object of our faith (Rom. 6:1-14; 8:1-11; I Cor. 1:17, 18-23; 2:2; Gal. 6:14; Col. 2:10-15; Phil. 3:17-19).

## DEATH TO SELF

Let us first look at death to self. The Scripture says, *"Make thee sharp knives, and circumcise again the children of Israel the second time."*

The battle with self is never ended once and for all, at least it will not be ended until the trump sounds or until the Lord calls us home. We would like for this battle to end, and at times we may foolishly think that it has; however, self keeps cropping up. It is a constant conflict between the flesh and the Spirit, hence, the words, *"the second time."* The death to self is illustrated in circumcision.

This rite was a sign of separation. Of course, the question is asked, separation from what? It is separation from dependence on self. In fact, we are a "self" and will always be a "self", but we are to never depend on self, but rather on the Holy Spirit. This is God's way. Most of the time when we think of separation, we are thinking of separation from the world. It certainly does include that. The world is an enemy to the child of God; however, our biggest enemy, of which circumcision is a type, is self. What type of self are we addressing?

Strangely enough, the self part of man that must be separated by the Spirit of God (circumcised) is that which we would call good. It is man's natural wisdom and goodness. It is most bitter for a man to learn that all of his goodness must be slain with the sword of the Lord just as much as all of his badness. However, this is most sweet to the Christian, for it brings him into a resurrection life, and the power of that life takes all strength from Satan (Rom. 6:5).

## THE CROSS OF CHRIST

*For the children of Israel walked forty years in the wilderness, till all the people who were men of war, which came out of Egypt,*

> *were consumed, because they obeyed not the voice of the* LORD: *unto whom the* LORD *sware that He would not shew them the land, which the* LORD *sware unto their fathers that He would give us, a land that floweth with milk and honey. And their children, whom he raised up in their stead, them Joshua circumcised: for they were uncircumcised, because they had not circumcised them by the way. And it came to pass, when they had done circumcising all the people, that they abode in their places in the camp, till they were whole. And the* LORD *said unto Joshua, This day have I rolled away the reproach of Egypt from off you. Wherefore the name of the place is called Gilgal unto this day* (Josh. 5:6-9).

It was all done at the cross. As we have previously stated, there Jesus died that we might be saved from sin but, as well, from self. Therefore, we are to look to the cross exclusively and understand that it is there where all victory was won (Col. 2:14-15). This means that the believer must anchor his faith exclusively in Christ and the cross and never allow it to be moved anywhere else. It is the cross, the cross, the cross!

## NO CONFIDENCE IN THE FLESH

Regardless of man's religion or his goodness, he has no strength, personally speaking, against Satan. Jericho's walls never fall before him. However, if death to all whom we think of as good, wise, and beautiful is suffered, it then becomes a shelter, for what can Satan do with a dead man? Paul said, *"We are the circumcision ... And have no confidence in the flesh"* (Phil. 3:3).

Circumcision, in fact, is a type of the cross and what Jesus did there:

- The sharp knife is applied to the male member, which is a picture of what the cross does to us in totality; however, we must die, of which the knife is a type, and which we do die with Christ at Calvary. We are *"baptized into his death ... We are buried with him by baptism into death,"* and *"By the glory of the Father ... We also should walk* (are raised with Him) *in newness of life"* (Rom. 6:3-4).

- Upon the knife performing the circumcision, blood is spilled, which is a type of the blood shed at Calvary's cross, and done so by our Lord and Savior Jesus Christ. As we die only in Him, as well, our blood is shed only in Him.

- Circumcision was the physical sign of the great covenant of God between Himself and His people. As stated, it was a physical picture of the cross. It is no longer mandatory for the male population of believers to be circumcised simply because Christ has fulfilled all the demands at Calvary's cross. In other words, we now have a better covenant based on better promises (Heb. 8:6-8).

## THE PASSOVER

*"And the children of Israel encamped in Gilgal, and kept the Passover on the fourteenth day of the month at evening in the plains of Jericho"* (Josh. 5:10).

This was the first Passover in the promised land. Israel eating the Passover proclaims that her redemption out of Egypt and her position in the land of Promise were alike due to the preciousness of the blood of the Lamb.

True spiritual victories can only be won where there is this testimony to the person and work of the Lord Jesus Christ. Circumcision, in symbolizing the cross, also symbolized the death of self. The Passover symbolizing the cross presents a testimony to the blood of the Lamb.

Joshua 5:10 says, *"And kept the Passover."* Israel proclaimed her redemption out of Egypt and her position in the land of Promise by keeping the Passover. We presently proclaim our redemption and dwelling because of the preciousness of the blood of the Paschal Lamb. That is the reason that Paul, with all of his education and worldly knowledge, said, *"I determined not to know any thing among you, save Jesus Christ, and him crucified"* (I Cor. 2:2).

Why?

## THE POWER OF THE SHED
## BLOOD OF JESUS CHRIST

The terrible bondages of humanity cannot be broken by the intellect, earthly wisdom, money, prestige, or education. It can only be broken by the power of the shed blood of Jesus Christ. That was Israel's victory then; it is our victory now. It is ever the cross!

A description of the Passover is given in Exodus 12. It is a perfect type of the cross.

It seems that Israel kept the Passover only one time in the wilderness, which was about a year after deliverance from Egypt (Num. 9:1-14). Now that they were to enter the promised land, they must enter by the power of the blood of the Lamb, symbolized by the Passover. This proclaimed Israel's strength. It was not their standing army or their military strategy, but rather their dependence on the shed blood of the Lamb. We must never forget that because our strength is the same presently.

I am saddened by the thought that the modern church is leaving the cross. To do so not only invites destruction but, in fact, is destruction. The only defense against the powers of darkness is the cross of Christ. With the cross laid aside, there is no defense, and wreckage is the result, and it's the most horrifying type of wreckage. We might as well say that the only thing standing between mankind and eternal hell is the cross of Christ. That is a sobering statement, but it is true.

When we walk through the gate of pearl in that city built foursquare, we will be there solely and completely because of Jesus and what He did at the cross. We must never forget that.

## THE WORD OF THE LORD

*"And they did eat of the old corn of the land on the morrow after the Passover, unleavened cakes, and parched corn in the selfsame day. And the manna ceased on the morrow after they had eaten of the old corn of the land; neither had the children of Israel manna anymore; but they did eat of the fruit of the land of Canaan that year"* (Josh. 5:11-12).

Manna was angel's food. It was sufficient for the wilderness and its defective spiritual life; however, the *"old corn of the land"* symbolized the Word of God, and it is a necessity for the strength needed for spiritual conquests. Everything must be by the Word.

The phrase, *"And they did eat of the old corn of the land,"* presents the first time this is mentioned. In fact, and as stated, for some forty years, Israel had existed on manna, which was angel's food. But now, since they were in the land, the strong meat of the Word was now needed. It is a must regarding the strength needed for spiritual conquests in the land of our inheritance.

———◇———

*All things are possible to him*
*That can in Jesus' name believe;*
*Lord, I no more Thy name blaspheme,*
*Thy truth I lovingly receive.*
*I can, I do believe in Thee;*
*All things are possible to me.*

*'Twas most impossible of all*
*That here sin's reign in me should cease;*
*Yet shall it be, I know it shall;*
*Jesus, I trust thy faithfulness.*
*If nothing is too hard for Thee,*
*All things are possible to me.*

*Though earth and hell the Word gainsay,*
*The Word of God shall never fail;*
*The Lord can break sin's iron sway;*
*'Tis certain, though impossible.*
*The thing impossible shall be,*
*All things are possible to me.*

*All things are possible to God;*
*To Christ, the power of God in man;*
*To me when I am all renewed,*
*In Christ am fully formed again,*
*And from the reign of sin set free,*
*All things are possible to me.*

*All things are possible to God;*
*To Christ, the power of God in me;*
*Now shed Thy mighty self abroad,*
*Let me no longer live, but Thee;*
*Give me this hour in Thee to prove*
*The sweet omnipotence of love.*

# RAHAB

## AND OTHER

# MIRACLES

## GOD'S PLAN FOR THE
## FALL OF JERICHO

# GOD'S PLAN FOR THE FALL OF JERICHO

## JESUS CHRIST AND HIM CRUCIFIED

The Bible is still one of, if not the, best-selling books in the world, but, regrettably and sadly, it is little read and meditated thereon. In fact, the present church is almost a Bibleless family. Most of the preaching today is psychology in one form or the other. In fact, the church has become so psychologized that I think most preachers little know or realize that they really aren't preaching the Word, but rather mouthing psychological jargon. It appeals to the flesh, but let it ever be understood that if it's not the Word of God, then it will do no good. Of course, when we speak of the Word of God, we mean the pure Word of God, which means it hasn't been polluted or perverted by the additives of the world. To pull it down to the so-called bottom line, if the message is not Jesus Christ and Him crucified, in other words, the cross, then it's not really the gospel.

## THE CROSS OF CHRIST

Paul said, *"For Christ sent me not to baptize* (presents to us a cardinal truth), *but to preach the gospel* (the manner in which one may be saved from sin): *not with wisdom of words* (intellectualism is not the gospel), *lest the cross of Christ should be made of none effect.* (This tells us in no uncertain terms that the cross of Christ must always be the emphasis of the message.)" (I Cor. 1:17). – The Expositor's Study Bible

In this one verse, we are plainly and clearly told what the gospel of Jesus Christ actually is—it is the cross of Christ. This means that the preacher must preach Christ as the source of all things from God and the cross as the means by which all of these things are given to us. It doesn't matter how clever the sermon might be, how glib it might be, or how intellectual it might seem to be. If anything other than the cross is preached, it will bring no good news to the poor, heal no broken hearts, bring no deliverance to captives, recover no sight for the blind, and it will not set at liberty them who are bruised (Luke 4:18)

## CAPTAIN OF THE HOST OF THE LORD

*And it came to pass, when Joshua was by Jericho, that he lifted up his eyes and looked, and, behold, there stood a man over against him with his sword drawn in his hand: and Joshua went unto him, and said unto him, Art thou for us, or for our adversaries? And he said, Nay; but as captain of the host of the LORD am I now come. And Joshua fell on his face to*

> the earth, and did worship, and said unto him, What saith
> my LORD unto his servant? And the captain of the LORD's
> Host said unto Joshua, Loose thy shoe from off your foot; for
> the place whereon thou standest is holy. And Joshua did so.
> (Josh. 5:13-15).

The *"man"* of verse 13 was a preincarnate appearance of
Christ, whom Joshua at first didn't recognize. When the Lord
revealed Himself, Joshua then recognized Him as the Lord.
Concerning this, Williams says, "An absolute condition of
victory is full surrender to Christ as Lord. He must be accepted
as captain, be permitted to plan, and be fully obeyed."[1]

The demand that the shoes be removed from Joshua's
feet, and the removal of those shoes, guaranteed that He who
now spoke to Joshua was a divine person, actually, as stated, a
preincarnate appearance of Christ. The removal of the shoes, in
essence, indicated that Joshua was giving up all ownership and
leadership and, thereby, giving Christ total control.

We have four steps to victory listed:
1. The death of self (circumcision)
2. Testimony to the blood of the Lamb (Passover)
3. Feeding on the Word of God (old corn of the land)
4. Subjection to Christ as Lord (pulling off the shoes)

## SUBMISSION TO CHRIST

There must be a full surrender to Christ in all things, which
can only be done by the believer going to the cross (Luke 9:23).

While in the wilderness, Egypt reproached Israel with a taunt that Jehovah could not bring them into the promised land. Furthermore, all of Egypt that attaches itself to a servant of God is a reproach to Him. Joshua would yield total authority to the *"captain"* as he *"fell on his face to the earth, and did worship."* He would then ask the question, *"What saith my* LORD *unto his servant?"* The answer would be startling.

At the beginning of His command, the Lord would not mention the conquest of Jericho, the great victories to be won, or all the great things He would do for Israel. He merely said, *"Loose thy shoes from off thy foot; for the place whereon you stand is holy."*

Unfortunately, the modern child of God is so busy seeking riches, etc., that he seldom seeks that which is the most important. The most important is that which is holy. How many thousands of preachers are trying to defeat the Evil One when they have never met the captain or stood on that which is holy?

This is the secret of the church: It is not the subjection of the Jerichos or the defeat of the Amorites and the Canaanites. It is first seeing Jesus in that which is holy. Then and only then will the Jerichos fall and the Amorites and the Canaanites be defeated.

In Joshua 5:9, the Lord said, *"This day have I rolled away the reproach of Egypt from off you,"* and this can only get done as we follow the captain. We cannot roll that reproach away from ourselves or of ourselves, only the captain can. As well, He does such by and through the cross, and only by and through the cross!

## SEVEN

> *Now Jericho was straitly shut up because of the children of Israel: none went out, and none came in. And the LORD said unto Joshua: See, I have given into thine hand Jericho, and the king thereof, and the mighty men of valour. And ye shall compass the city, all ye men of war, and go round about the city once. Thus shalt you do six days. And seven priests shall bear before the ark seven trumpets of rams' horns: and the seventh day ye shall compass the city seven times, and the priests shall blow with the trumpets* (Josh. 6:1-4).

The strong fortress of Jericho barred Israel's entrance to the land. Satan will always have such a fortress to hinder our spiritual progress.

It was, in fact, impregnable; therefore, its conquest was impossible to Israel, but not impossible to God.

What the Lord told Joshua to do as it regarded the taking of Jericho was probably the strangest plan of battle ever formed.

The number seven as used here, is not without purpose and design. Biblically, the number symbolizes perfection, totality, and universality. These are God's plans, and they always succeed. We should cease to make plans for ourselves and let God plan for us. As stated, His plans always succeed.

The Lord plainly told Joshua, *"See, I have given into thine hand Jericho."* However, I might quickly add that this was only if Joshua followed totally the instructions given by the Lord. That's our major problem presently. We either try to formulate the plans ourselves, or else, we do not follow the plans that God has laid out. The Lord gave Joshua instructions. To the natural mind, they would be foolish: *"Go round about the city once. Thus shalt thou do six days."*

If one would notice, in verse 4, the number seven is used repeatedly. There are seven priests, seven trumpets, the seventh day and then seven times. Why all these sevens?

Everything in the Word of God is for an express purpose. Nothing is done for show or selfish occupation. All have tremendous spiritual meaning.

## SPIRITUAL INSTRUCTIONS OF FAITH

As previously stated, in the Word of God, the number seven is God's number. It denotes perfection, completion, totality, universality, and all in all. It must be remembered that Joshua is operating strictly in the spiritual sense. Regrettably, all too often we modern Christians operate in the worldly sense. We borrow our ideas from the world, insert them into that which is called Christianity, and pass it off as the Word of God. God will have none of it.

These are spiritual instructions of faith. The world, the natural mind, or Jericho will have absolutely no idea what they mean as the natural mind cannot understand *"the things of the Spirit"* (I Cor. 2:14).

Regrettably, most in the modern church have little or no knowledge at all of the things of the Spirit; they only understand the things of the world.

## INSTRUCTIONS

> *And it shall come to pass, that when they make a long blast with the ram's horn, and when ye hear the sound of the trumpet, all the people shall shout with a great shout; and the wall of the city shall fall down flat, and the people shall ascend up every man straight before him. And Joshua the son of Nun called the priests, and said unto them, Take up the ark of the covenant, and let seven priests bear seven trumpets of rams' horns before the ark of the LORD. And he said unto the people, Pass on, and compass the city, and let him who is armed pass on before the ark of the LORD. And it came to pass, when Joshua had spoken unto the people, that the seven priests bearing the seven trumpets of rams' horns passed on before the LORD, and blew with the trumpets: and the ark of the covenant of the LORD followed them* (Josh. 6:5-8).

## THE ARK OF THE COVENANT

Why were the seven priests with the seven rams' horns placed before the ark? Why wasn't the ark first?

The priests were types of Christ. The ark of the covenant was a type of the very throne of God. The idea is that Christ is the one who has defeated the enemy, and He has done so by going to the cross. He is the way, and the only way, to the very throne of God. Therefore, the seven priests with their rams' horns going before the ark was, in essence, a statement that said that Jesus would one day open up the way to the very throne of God. This He most definitely did at Calvary's cross. As stated, every single thing done here has a scriptural and spiritual meaning. If we understand that meaning, we will understand God's prescribed order of victory. That prescribed order is always the cross of Christ.

The Lord didn't need Israel to march around Jericho seven days, or even one day, for the walls to fall down. So, why did He have them do this?

It was to teach them trust, dependence on Him, and obedience, even though they did not at all understand the directions, as neither would anyone. However, understanding what the Lord is doing is not necessarily the criterion— obedience is!

As a military maneuver, all of this marching was worse than useless; however, it was not a military maneuver, but rather that which was spiritual.

## DO NOT MAKE ANY NOISE

*And the armed men went before the priests that blew with the trumpets, and the rereward came after the ark, the priests going on, and blowing with the trumpets. And Joshua had commanded the people, saying, Ye shall not shout, nor make any noise with your voice, neither shall any word proceed out of your mouth, until the day I bid you shout; then shall ye shout. So the ark of the LORD compassed the city, going about it once: and they came into the camp, and lodged in the camp. And Joshua rose early in the morning, and the priests took up the ark of the LORD (Josh. 6:9-12).*

## THE LORD HAS CHOSEN THAT HE
## WORK THROUGH BELIEVERS

That is His plan. If there are no men or women for Him to work through, the work of God is not done. The ark of God would only follow godly, consecrated, and holy men—and here is where we make our mistake. Men are not necessarily holy because of what they do. They are holy because of what Jesus has done. We speak of the cross and our faith in Him and the work that He has accomplished by the giving of Himself as a sacrifice.

Some think that because someone has failed, he is, thereby, unholy. If he has repented, however, there is no unholiness left. To be frank with you, there are no human beings who ever existed who have not failed: *"For all have sinned and come short of the glory of God"* (Rom. 3:23).

Now, this is not merely speaking of the past tense. The Greek text bears it out that all of us, even the best of us, are continually coming short of the glory of God. If you don't know that, then you really don't know yourself or the grace of God.

God certainly places no premium on failure; however if lack of failure is a criterion for being used of God, then the Bible greats could never have been used. So, if you are allowing Satan (or men) to tell you that because you have failed, you can never be used of God again, please remember this: The ones telling you this have failed over and over again and are now doing the service of Satan by mouthing their unbelief. The failure of not believing is the only failure that will prohibit an individual from marching around Jericho and ultimately blowing the victory note on the rams' horns and being followed by the ark of the Lord. Regrettably, most of the modern church is riddled with that failure.

## SHOUT

*And seven priests bearing seven trumpets of rams' horns before the ark of the LORD went on continually, and blew with the trumpets: and the armed men went before them; but the rereward came after the ark of the Lord, the priests going on, and blowing with the trumpets. And the second day they compassed the city once, and returned into the camp: so they did six days. And it came to pass on the seventh day, that they rose early about the dawning of the day, and compassed the city after the same manner seven times: only on that day they compassed the city seven times. And it came to pass at the seventh time, when the priests blew with the trumpets, Joshua said unto the people, Shout; for the LORD has given you the city (Josh. 6:13-16).*

The people of God were to march around the walls of Jericho once a day for six days, and they were to make no sound at all.

Seven priests were to lead the procession, and the ark of the covenant, borne on the shoulders of priests, was to follow them. The only noise that was to be made was by the priests blowing on the trumpets, which they did.

## THE SEVENTH DAY

Now comes the seventh day. On that day they were to march around the walls seven times, whereas the previous six days they had marched just one time a day. Even though the trumpets were blown by the priests all six days, and the people were to make no sound at all during that time, this must have been a strange procession to those on the other side of the walls of Jericho.

The order seems to have been: armed men went first, followed by the priests, and then the ark of the covenant.

Now, on the seventh day after they had marched six times around the walls, when they started on the seventh time, the priests blew with the trumpets and *"Joshua said unto the people, Shout; for the LORD has given you the city."*

Please understand that all of these things had no military bearing on Jericho whatsoever, but it had a great spiritual bearing.

## THE ACCURSED CITY

*And the city shall be accursed, even it, and all that are therein, to the LORD: only Rahab the harlot shall live, she and all who are with her in the house, because she hid the messengers that we sent. And ye, in any wise keep yourselves from the accursed thing, lest ye make yourselves accursed, when ye take of the accursed thing, and make the camp of Israel a curse, and trouble it. But all the silver, and gold, and vessels of brass and iron, are consecrated unto the LORD: they shall come into the treasury of the LORD* (Josh. 6:17-19).

As it regards verse 18, unfortunately, there was one man who didn't obey, which caused Israel great trouble. Everything about the city was cursed by God because it was wholly given over to idol worship. The modern Christian, likewise, must be very careful about his entanglement with the world. While we are *in* the world, we are not to be *of* the world. In fact, if the world gets into the believer, it is the same as water getting into a ship. Ruin is the result!

## SHOUT

Going back to Joshua 6:10, it says two things:
1. *"Ye shall not shout."*
2. *"Then shall ye shout."*

We are told here in the Word of God that there is a time to shout and a time not to shout. Why could they not shout at the beginning?

Millions today in Christendom are shouting when there is actually nothing to shout about. They have not heard from heaven. They have not seen the captain of the Lord of Hosts. They have not pulled off their shoes or stood on holy ground. Faith doesn't have to scream to make itself heard. So many trumpet the loudness of their profession to cover up the bareness of their possession. In fact, much of the shouting in modern churches is superficial, hollow, and only on the surface. So, when should we shout?

The Scripture says, *"Then,"* which means after we have obeyed the Lord and done exactly what He has told us to do.

I think one can say without fear of scriptural contradiction that the criterion for the shout is that one's faith be placed exclusively in Christ and what Christ has done for us at the cross (Rom. 6:1-14; 8:1-11; I Cor. 1:17-18, 21, 23; 2:2; Col. 2:10-15).

## THE CROSS OF CHRIST AND THE SHOUT OF VICTORY

The reason the shout of victory is placed exclusively in the cross of Christ is simply because it was at the cross where total and complete victory was won, and for all time. Everything about the description given in this chapter points to the cross of Christ.

- The number seven (God's number of perfection) of Joshua 6:4 points exclusively to a perfect salvation, which is afforded by Christ and what He did at the cross.
- Seven priests went before the ark blowing seven trumpets, all signifying Christ and what He would do to redeem humanity, which was done by the means of the cross.
- The shout signified victory by faith. If it is to be noticed, they shouted before the walls fell down and not after. In fact, it's easy to shout after the victory, but it takes real faith to shout before the victory is evident.

Considering what Jesus did at the cross, there is a shout of victory in the cross, and, in fact, the shout of victory is found only in the cross. Everything else is superficial, hollow, shallow, and without substance.

## THE GREAT SHOUT

*"So the people shouted when the priests blew with the trumpets: and it came to pass, when the people heard the sound of the trumpet, and the people shouted with a great shout, that the wall fell down flat, so that the people went up into the city, every man straight before him, and they took the city. And they utterly destroyed all that was in the city, both man and woman, young and old, and ox, and sheep, and ass, with the edge of the sword"* ( Josh. 6:20-21).

Had Israel attempted to take Jericho without the leading of the Lord, casualties would have been great.

Following the Lord, there is no record that there were any casualties whatsoever among the army of Israel.

The army of Israel was commanded to kill all the people in the city, even the children. This was because the city was wholly given over to idolatry, with all of its attendant immorality, which was gross to say the least. All—with the exception of Rahab and her family—were to be killed.

One archaeologist said sometime back that the God of the Old Testament who gave instructions for the entire tribes to be eliminated, including the children, etc., did future generations an untold service. They had sunk so deeply into sin and perversion that God was forced to conduct major surgery.

Even though the little children below the age of accountability were executed, still, every evidence is that their souls and their spirits at death went to be with the Lord. These children born of parents of unspeakable perversion were tainted at birth so powerfully that execution was necessary.

## THE FALL OF JERICHO

Joshua 6:20 says, *"They took the city."* As stated, there is no record that even one Israelite was lost. This is God's way. Sometimes we win great victories, albeit with great loss. This is a sure sign that much flesh has been associated with what little of the Holy Spirit we have allowed to function; consequently, that is why we suffer loss.

Here there is no loss at all, *"They took the city."* The reason that there was no loss is obvious: they followed the instructions of faith to the letter.

## THE LEADING OF THE SPIRIT

Believers reading the Old Testament and the account of these tremendous miracles seem to think at times that it was easier then than now. In other words, it was easier then for people to believe and see God do great things than at the present time. That is not so!

In fact, since the cross, the Holy Spirit now abides in the hearts and lives of all believers, and does so permanently. He is there for the express purpose of serving as our helper. To be sure, His leading and guidance is far more pronounced presently than at former times. Jesus said:

> *Howbeit when He, the Spirit of truth, is come* (which He did on the day of Pentecost), *He will guide you into all truth* (if our faith is properly placed in Christ and the cross, the Holy

Spirit can then bring forth truth to us; He doesn't guide into some truth, but rather 'all truth'): *for He shall not speak of Himself* (tells us not only what He does, but whom He represents); *but whatsoever He shall hear, that shall He speak* (doesn't refer to lack of knowledge, for the Holy Spirit is God, but rather He will proclaim the work of Christ only): *and He will show you things to come* (pertains to the new covenant, which would shortly be given) (John. 16:13) – The Expositor's Study Bible

## A BETTER COVENANT

In fact, concerning this very thing, Paul said:

*But now* (since the cross) *has He* (the Lord Jesus) *obtained a more excellent ministry* (the new covenant in Jesus' blood is superior and takes the place of the old covenant in animal blood), *by how much also He is the mediator of a better covenant* (proclaims the fact that Christ officiates between God and man according to the arrangements of the new covenant), *which was established upon better promises.* (This presents the new covenant explicitly based on the cleansing and forgiveness of all sin, which the old covenant could not do.) *For if that first covenant had been faultless* (proclaims the fact that the first covenant was definitely not faultless; as stated, it was based on animal blood, which was vastly inferior to the precious blood of Christ), *then should no place have been sought for the second* (proclaims the necessity of the new covenant). *For finding fault with them* (the first covenant was actually designed to glaringly portray the fault of the people, which it successfully did), *He said* (Jer. 31:31), *Behold, the days come, saith the Lord, when I will make a new covenant with the house of Israel and with the house of Judah* (that new covenant was in Christ and what He did at the cross; regrettably, Israel rejected Him) (Heb. 8:6-8) – The Expositor's Study Bible

## THE SPIRIT OF TRUTH

There are some miracles that God performed in Old Testament times that He has not repeated, but only because there is not the necessity of such at present. For example, God opened the Red Sea, but considering all the events that transpired, there hasn't been a need to do such again.

The Holy Spirit was *with* a person before the cross because that's all He could be. After the cross, He is *in* a person. However, there is a great difference in Him being *with* a person than being *in* that person, residing permanently and, therefore, helping him constantly. Jesus said so:

*Even the Spirit of truth* (the Greek says, 'The Spirit of the truth,' which refers to the Word of God; actually, He does far more than merely superintend the attribute of truth, as Christ 'is truth' [1 John 5:6]); *whom the world cannot receive* (the Holy Spirit cannot come into the heart of the unbeliever until that person makes Christ his or her Saviour; then He comes in), *because it sees Him not, neither knows Him* (refers to the fact that only born-again believers can understand the Holy Spirit and know Him): *but you know Him* (would have been better translated, 'But you shall get to know Him'); *for He dwells with you* (before the cross), *and shall be in you* (this would take place on the day of Pentecost and forward because the sin debt has been forever paid by Christ on the cross, changing the disposition of everything) (John 14:17) – The Expositor's Study Bible

## LEADING AND GUIDANCE

The truth is, if we as believers will fully consecrate ourselves, make certain that our faith is anchored properly in Christ and the cross, and do not allow it to be moved elsewhere, to be sure, the Holy Spirit will then lead us and guide us to a far greater degree.

He wants to help! He wants to lead! He wants to guide! He wants to empower! However, oftentimes we do things that are totally contrary to the Word of God, which greatly hinders the Holy Spirit and His work within our hearts and lives, as should be obvious.

For instance, sadly and regrettably, most Christians have their faith placed in anything and everything except Christ and the cross. In fact, most Christians understand the cross not at all as it regards their sanctification—their everyday living for God. As a result, whether they realize it or not, they are actually living in a state of spiritual adultery, which greatly hinders the Holy Spirit and what He can do (Rom. 7:1-4).

## TOTAL DESTRUCTION OF THE ENEMY

Joshua 6:21 says, *"And they utterly destroyed all."*

To properly understand this verse, we must bring it over into the new covenant and into our everyday life and living for the Lord.

This means that every vestige of temper, jealousy, ambition, pride, deceit, envy, etc., must be utterly destroyed in our lives. There must be nothing there of the flesh. However, the problem is this: We try to destroy the flesh with the flesh and fail as ever we must. Flesh cannot destroy flesh. Sickness cannot heal sickness. Sin cannot save from sin. All the rules of legalism in our churches cannot set one captive free. It can make evident more sin, which is the last thing we want, but legalism (the flesh) cannot set anyone free. Yet, when the Spirit of God has His perfect and complete way, all is utterly destroyed.

## THE FLESH

Paul used the term *"the flesh"* over and over (Rom. 8:1, 3-5). In fact, he said, *"So then they that are in the flesh cannot please God"* (Rom. 8:8).

The Holy Spirit through the apostle used the term *flesh* to describe human capabilities, intellectualism, personal education, knowledge, ability, power, talent, willpower, etc. Within themselves, these things aren't necessarily wrong; however, the wrong comes in when we try to live for God by the means of the flesh, in other words, by our own capabilities.

It simply cannot be done. When we attempt to live for God after this fashion, this greatly insults Christ. Even as Paul said, such an effort greatly displeases the Lord.

## WHY?

Despite what we think, it is impossible for the believer to live for God, work for God, experience the fruit of the Spirit, or grow in grace and the knowledge of the Lord by the means of the flesh. It cannot be done. But this is where the church runs aground and, in fact, where all of us at one time or another have run aground. The church keeps coming up with one fad after another, with all proposing to develop something in our lives. A perfect example is *The Purpose Driven Life*, which is all of the flesh and will bring about no positive results whatsoever. These fads invariably turn out to be of no avail. There is only one way that the believer can successfully live for the Lord.

## GOD'S PRESCRIBED ORDER OF VICTORY

If it is to be noticed, I have used this subheading, "God's Prescribed Order of Victory," several times already. I do it for a purpose. It is so important that I want you, the reader, to know perfectly well what the Bible teaches as it regards our living for the Lord. Nothing could be more important. Even though it is repetitive, it is worth reading and studying several times. Read the following very carefully:

- Focus: the Lord Jesus Christ (John 14:6);
- Object of faith: the cross of Christ (Rom. 6:1-14; Col. 2:10-15);
- Power source: the Holy Spirit (Rom. 8:1-11);
- Results: victory (Rom. 6:14).

Even though what we have given is extremely abbreviated, if you, the believer, will meditate on this little short diagram and ask the Holy Spirit to give you leading and guidance, it will begin to become crystal clear. It tells us in abbreviated form how to live for God.

However, let's look at it again from the way this little formula is used by most modern Christians.

- Focus: works!
- Object of faith: performance!
- Power source: self!
- Results: defeat!

## WHY IS THE CROSS OF CHRIST SO IMPORTANT?

It is because the Bible says so. (Gen. 3:15; Ex. 12:13; Isa. 53; Rom. 6:1-14; I Cor. 1:17-18, 21, 23; 2:2; Gal. 5; 6:14; Eph. 2:13-18; Phil. 3:17-19; Col. 2:10-15).

It was at the cross that all sin was atoned. Because of all sin being atoned, Satan and all of his cohorts—fallen angels, demon spirits—were defeated (Col. 2:14-15). Sin is the legal means that Satan has to hold mankind in bondage. With all sin atoned, which it was at Calvary's cross, Satan has lost that legal right; consequently, he can place men presently in bondage only by the consent of the governed. What do we mean by that?

The unredeemed person gives Satan consent to place him in bondage by refusing Jesus Christ. There is no other hope except Christ. Regrettably, believers do the same identical thing when they place their faith in something other than the cross of Christ. Let us say it again as we've already said any number of times: Christ is the source of everything we receive from God, whatever it might be, while the cross is the legal means by which it is given to us (Rom. 8:2).

Much of the modern church preaches Jesus but without the cross. Some do so out of ignorance, and some do so out of unbelief. Either way, the damage is done!

It was to the apostle Paul that the meaning of the new covenant was given (Gal. 1:1-12). In fact, the meaning of the new covenant is actually the meaning of the cross, even as the meaning of the cross is the meaning of the new covenant.

In graphic form, Paul also gave this to us in his description of the Lord's Supper, which characterizes and epitomizes the new covenant. Actually, Jesus is the new covenant, meaning that He doesn't merely have the new covenant but, in reality, is the new covenant. It's ours because of the cross (I Cor. 11:24-34).

## JESUS CHRIST AND HIM CRUCIFIED

That's the reason that we boldly declare that *The Purpose Driven Life* scheme is not of God. This tale does not hold up Christ and the cross but rather works of the law (laws devised by men). I'm sure that the writer of this book would vehemently deny that his efforts constitute nothing but law; however, the following must be recognized, that is, if we are to be scriptural.

If we aren't preaching Jesus Christ and Him crucified (the cross), then pure and simple, whatever it is we are preaching and teaching has to be law. There are only two places that the believer can be—grace or law. If we are functioning in grace, we can only do so by our faith being placed squarely in Christ and the cross. Everything else constitutes law. So, when believers claim that they are functioning in grace when, in fact, they are omitting and ignoring the cross, it places them in an unscriptural position, despite their claims.

Paul said, *"For Christ sent me not to baptize, but to preach the gospel: not with wisdom of words, lest the cross of Christ should be made of none effect. For the preaching of the cross is to them who perish foolishness; but unto us which are saved it is the power of God"* (I Cor. 1:17-18).

Finally, the apostle said, *"For I determined not to know any thing among you, save Jesus Christ, and him crucified"* (I Cor. 2:2).

Paul's statement plainly tells us that with purpose and design, he did not resort to the knowledge or philosophy of the world regarding the preaching of the gospel. He preached the cross as the answer to man's dilemma, and the cross alone as the answer to man's dilemma! That and that alone is the message that will save the sinner, set the captive free, and give the believer perpetual victory.

## RAHAB

> But Joshua had said unto the two men that had spied
> out the country, Go into the harlot's house, and bring out thence
> the woman, and all that she hath, as ye swore unto her. And the
> young men that were spies went in, and brought out Rahab, and
> her father, and her mother, and her brethren, and all that she
> had; and they brought out all her kindred, and left them without
> the camp of Israel. And they burnt the city with fire, and all
> that was therein: only the silver, and the gold, and the vessels
> of brass and of iron, they put into the treasury of the house of
> the LORD. And Joshua saved Rahab the harlot alive, and her
> father's household, and all that she had; and she dwelleth in
> Israel even unto this day; because she hid the messengers, which
> Joshua sent to spy out Jericho (Josh. 6:22-25).

The story of this dear lady is one of the grandest in all of
biblical history. A poor lost daughter of Adam's fallen race, even
having given over her life to total licentiousness, she was made
an example of grace simply because of her faith in Christ. She
and her family were the only ones in the entirety of the city of
Jericho who took advantage of the grace of God. If the leaders
of Jericho had come to Joshua and stated that they wished to
accept Israel's God, namely Jehovah, and, thereby, rejected their
heathenistic idols, they would have been spared exactly as were
Rahab and her family. They did not do that and were totally lost!

Rahab is a type of the entirety of the human race—lost,
heathenistic, without God, and without hope—but faith

brought her out of this morass of sin and shame exactly as faith has brought out untold millions.

## SALVATION

Williams said, "Salvation by the scarlet cord was not only simple, it was also sure. When this day of wrath came, it gave the safety it promised. Thus will it be in the day of the wrath to come. That day will prove how sure is the salvation which follows upon simply trusting Jesus."[2]

Although slated for destruction, the faith of Rahab saved her. Rahab married Salmon, one of the princes of Israel. She is included in our Lord's genealogy (Matt. 1:5). To what heights of glory her faith took her, and so may it be for all who will dare to believe God. The Lord took her harlotry and turned it into holiness. He took the curse that was upon her and turned it into a blessing. What He did for her, He will do for you and me as well. The entirety of the family of Rahab was saved because the entirety of her family placed themselves under the protection of the shed blood of the lamb, typified by the red cord.

## THE WRATH OF GOD

The modern church has almost totally set aside the great biblical truth of the wrath of God, typified in the destruction of Jericho. However, let the following be understood: God is unalterably opposed to sin in every form! The Scripture plainly says:

*"For the wrath of God* (God's personal emotion with regard to sin) *is revealed from heaven* (this anger originates with God) *against all ungodliness and unrighteousness of men* (God must unalterably be opposed to sin)*, who hold the truth in unrighteousness* (who refuse to recognize who God is, and what God is)*"* (Rom. 1:18) – The Expositor's Study Bible.

As we have previously stated, the only thing standing between mankind and the wrath of God is the cross of Christ. Men may argue that His wrath is not now being evidenced. While that may be true in some cases, still, the term *wrath of God* actually speaks of man being condemned to eternal hell, and placed there forever and forever. If men refuse Christ and the cross, which is the only answer for sin, eternal hell will be the result. That is the wrath of God.

Jericho was totally destroyed, which typified the wrath of God against sin. As well, it typified what is going to happen to all who reject the Lord Jesus Christ. It may be awhile in coming, but come it shall (Rev. 20:11-15).

## JERICHO

*"And Joshua adjured them at that time, saying, Cursed be the man before the LORD, that riseth up and buildeth this city Jericho: he shall lay the foundation thereof in his firstborn, and in his youngest son shall he set up the gates of it. So the LORD was with Joshua; and his fame was noised throughout all the country"* (Josh. 6:26-27).

The object of this solemn pronouncement was to preserve Jericho as a spot devoted to God forever. For this reason a curse was pronounced upon anyone who should attempt to build a city upon the devoted spot.

It does not seem that it was forbidden to build habitations on the spot, for Jericho is frequently mentioned in the New Testament. What seems to have been forbidden was the erection of a fortified city.

This curse pronounced by Joshua actually fell on the reckless Hiel (1 Kings 16:34). He saw the laying of its foundation marked by the death of his eldest son, while the death of his youngest followed its completion.

*I know not why God's wondrous grace*
*To me He has made known,*
*Nor why, unworthy, Christ in love*
*Redeemed me for his own.*

# RAHAB

## AND OTHER

# MIRACLES

## TRESPASS

# TRESPASS

## THE ACCURSED THING

> *But the children of Israel committed a trespass in the accursed thing: for Achan, the son of Carmi, the son of Zabdi, the son of Zerah, of the tribe of Judah, took of the accursed thing: and the anger of the LORD was kindled against the children of Israel. And Joshua sent men from Jericho to Ai, which is beside Beth-aven, on the east side of Bethel, and spake unto them, saying, Go up and view the country. And the men went up and viewed Ai. And they returned to Joshua, and said unto him, Let not all the people go up; but let about two or three thousand men go up and smite Ai; and make not all the people to labour thither; for they are but few* (Josh. 7:1-3).

It doesn't seem that Joshua prayed about Ai. Had he done so, the sin would have been immediately discovered and defeat avoided. The danger after a victory is evident because of over-confidence. In such an atmosphere, it is easy to forget to pray.

Hidden sin was the cause of this failure. In the life of victory, God is the one and only strength of the believer; the believer has no other strength. However, God cannot give that strength if sin be indulged. If He did, He would deny His own nature, which is holiness. When He acts in power in the midst of His people, He must act in harmony with His own nature. Hence, He must judge sin in the camp of Israel with the same fierce anger with which He judged it in the city of Jericho. That judgment in both cases was death.

## DEFEAT

*"So there went up thither of the people about three thousand men: and they fled before the men of Ai. And the men of Ai smote of them about thirty and six men: for they chased them from before the gate even unto Shebarim, and smote them in the going down: wherefore the hearts of the people melted, and became as water. And Joshua rent his clothes, and fell to the earth upon his face before the ark of the LORD until the eventide, he and the elders of Israel, and put dust upon their heads"* (Josh. 7:4-6).

This narrative shows us the reason for failure in the life of the Christian—sin. As sin stopped the advance of God's people in the land of Promise, so sin will stop the advance of God's people today. God's holiness cannot abide sin. Likewise, God's grace cannot refuse forgiveness to those who will truly repent. Sadly, there is very little evidence that Achen repented.

However, if the discovery and judgment of sin is painful, and if there is faithfulness in dealing with it, then grace gives both blessing and victory, and the valley of Achor, which had been a valley of death, will now become a door of hope (Hos. 2:15). Sin must be feared, but neither its bitterness nor its punishment should be dreaded, for it is at this point that God resumes His victory—having fellowship with His child.

## WHAT IS REPENTANCE?

*Repentance* means "to turn about, to have a change of mind, to express regret." *Repentance*, used as a verb, means "the act of turning about," while *repentance*, used as a noun, means "the result of turning about."

True repentance actually refers to a basic change in man's attitude toward God. That attitude cannot actually be changed unless in some way it becomes a part of the cross of Christ. We have a picture of this at the very dawn of time, actually, on the first page of human history. It is the story of Cain and Abel.

The Lord had shown the first family that despite the terrible fall, they could have forgiveness of sins and communion with Him; however, it could only be by the means of the slain lamb, which was a representative of the Redeemer who would eventually come, the Lord Jesus Christ. Abel offered up the correct sacrifice and received that which God promised, while Cain rejected it, thereby, offering up his own sacrifice, which God could not accept. The end result was that Cain murdered his brother; therefore, at the very beginning, the foundation was laid for all that God does and the result of refusing that which He has given.

## THE ALTAR

Cain did not refuse to build an altar, and neither did he refuse to offer sacrifice. He just refused to offer the sacrifice that God demanded, which was an innocent victim, in essence, the lamb. The church, if we would use that term, has continued to follow this pattern down through the ages. Only a small part in the church has trusted in Christ and the cross, while the far greater majority has gone the way of Cain—offering up its own sacrifice—which God can never accept.

At this particular time, the problem is more acute than ever. I speak of *The Purpose Driven Life* scheme. I speak of the confession message, which completely denies the cross of Christ. I speak of denominationalism. Of course, there are a hundred and one other false directions that one could name as well. If it is looked at closely, it will be found that all of these schemes parrot that which was carried out by Cain so long, long ago. Man doesn't refuse to build an altar, and neither does he refuse to offer up sacrifice. He just wants to offer up a sacrifice of his own making.

## THE REVELATION OF THE CROSS

In 1997, after some six years of concentrated prayer both morning and night, the Lord began to open up to me the great revelation of the cross. To be sure, it was not anything new, but it was actually that which had been given to the apostle Paul. I was taken by the Holy Spirit directly to Romans 6 and 8.

This revelation has changed my life, my heart, my ministry, and, in fact, every facet of my life and living. I will forever thank the Lord, and, as the songwriter said, "The Old Rugged cross made the difference."

As this great revelation began to be opened up to me, to be sure, I could not wait to proclaim to the world what the Lord had given me. I speak primarily of the cross as it refers to sanctification. In other words, I speak of how we live for God on a daily basis, how we have victory over the world, the flesh, and the devil, and how we grow in grace and the knowledge of the Lord. In fact, this revelation continues to open up even unto this very hour.

I had labored in ignorance of this great truth all of my Christian experience, and this particular ignorance caused me untold failure, shame, and humiliation before the entirety of the world. However, as someone has well said, "Desperation always precedes revelation." I cannot guarantee that it always precedes revelation, but I know it happened with Paul, and I know it happened with me. The desperation definitely did precede the revelation.

## ACCEPTANCE?

At any rate, I couldn't wait to tell the story. I knew that the majority of the church world, even as I, was ignorant of the cross of Christ as it regarded sanctification. In other words, I knew that the body of Christ did not know or understand that the believer must have his faith anchored squarely in the cross of Christ in order for the Holy Spirit to work in his life to give him victory over the world, the flesh, and the devil. This is the only way that victory can be attained.

However, I found to my dismay that most were not interested. Then I found to my utter dismay that the cause and the reason was unbelief. Most in the modern church simply do not believe that what Jesus did at the cross answers man's dilemma, and does so in totality. Regrettably and sadly, it rather turns to its own schemes and fads, or most of all, to humanistic psychology. Thank God that some have accepted, are accepting, and I know shall accept, but as always and sadder still, the majority has gone by the way of Cain (Gen. 4).

## REPENTANCE WITHOUT THE CROSS!

Actually, repentance without the cross cannot really be effected as it should be. I refer basically to understanding the cross as it refers to our everyday living for God.

Let me explain: Most of the time, the sin that one commits is not really the problem. It is actually a symptom of the real problem. The tragedy is that most believers do not know or understand what the real problem is.

The real problem is man's rebellion against God's prescribed order of victory, which is Jesus Christ and Him crucified (I Cor. 1:23). In other words, if the believer has placed his faith in something other than Christ and the cross, then failure is inevitably going to be the result. In fact, it cannot be otherwise. The cross alone addresses sin. Nothing else does! So then, that's the real problem—faith placed in the wrong object.

However, if the believer doesn't know and understand that, his life will be one of sinning and repenting and sinning and repenting! I speak of those who are not hypocrites but truly know the Lord. Such a life doesn't exactly fall out to the abundance of which Jesus spoke (John 10:10).

So, the believer addresses himself to the failure, whatever it might be, but it's all to no avail. As stated, he is merely treating the symptom. He will find that this type of existence is little more than a merry-go-round, with the situation of sinning and repenting being repeated over and over again. Actually, it is because he is addressing the symptoms only and not the real cause.

## THE WORK OF THE HOLY SPIRIT

True repentance is the believer not only repenting of the bad he has committed, but the good as well! Now, what do we mean by repenting of the good?

By using the word *good,* we are referring to the flesh. We are referring to man's own ability, his own intelligence, his own prowess, and his own capabilities, which are all used, and in a good way at that, to try to overcome the world. Because these things are good, it fools us, but the truth is as follows: Man cannot effect within himself what needs to be effected. In other words, man cannot make himself righteous or holy, irrespective of who he is, how hard he tries, or how consecrated or dedicated to the Lord he might be. That might come as a shock to most. Many will read that and look at it in disbelief simply because man is always very proud of the flesh, and especially religious man.

Regarding this example, I quote Williams:

Isaac and Ishmael symbolized the new and the old nature in the believer. Sarah and Hagar typified the two covenants of works and grace, of bondage and liberty (Gal., Chpt. 4). The birth of the new nature demands the expulsion of the old. It is impossible to improve the old nature. The Holy Spirit says in Romans, Chapter 8, that 'it is enmity against God, that it is not subject to the law of God, neither indeed can be.' If therefore it cannot be subject to the law of God, how can the old nature be improved?

## MORAL EVOLUTION

Williams also said:

How foolish therefore appears the doctrine of moral evolution! The divine way of holiness is to 'put off the old man' just as Abraham 'put off Ishmael'. Man's way of holiness is to improve the 'old man,' that is, to improve Ishmael. The effort is both foolish and hopeless. Of course, the casting out of Ishmael was 'very grievous in Abraham's sight' because it always causes a struggle to cast out this element of bondage, that is salvation by works. For legalism is dear to the heart. Ishmael was the fruit, and to Abraham, the fair fruit of his own energy and planning.[1]

Therefore, Abraham did not give up Ishmael easily, and neither do we give up the works of our flesh easily either, especially the religious works.

However, they must all be given up, with our faith placed totally and completely in Christ and the cross, which then gives the Holy Spirit latitude to work in our hearts and lives. In that manner, and that manner only, can the believer walk in victory. That is God's way, and His only way! That's how we repent of the good, which, in effect, is the part of *"the tree of the knowledge of good and evil"* (Gen. 2:17). This is true repentance and is the only type of repentance that will fall out to victory—repentance with the cross of Christ as the foundation (I Cor. 1:17-18).

In the final analysis, the problem is not the Canaanites or what they will say or do, but the problem is sin. The only way to properly address sin is to take it to the cross. Unfortunately, the modern church is trying to address it with humanistic psychology or a bevy of schemes and fads, all psychologically laced.

Let us say it again: The only answer for sin is the cross!

## AND WHAT WILL YOU DO UNTO YOUR GREAT NAME?

*"And Joshua said, Alas, O LORD GOD, wherefore hast thou at all brought this people over Jordan, to deliver us into the hand of the Amorites, to destroy us? Would to God we had been content, and dwelt on the other side Jordan! O LORD, what shall I say, when Israel turneth their backs before their enemies! For the Canaanites and all the inhabitants of the land shall hear of it, and shall environ*

*us round, and cut off our name from the earth: and what wilt thou do unto thy great name?"* (Josh. 7:7-9).

Sin can be overcome in the life of the believer only by the believer looking exclusively to Christ and the cross. It is at the cross where sin was addressed, and only at the cross. When the believer places his or her faith exclusively in Christ and the cross (it must be in both), the Holy Spirit will then work mightily in the heart and life of such a believer and give total and complete victory (Rom. 6:1:14; 8:1-11; I Cor. 1:17-18, 21, 23; 2:2; Gal. 6:14; Col. 2:14-15).

It doesn't take very much for the faith of even the strongest saint, such as Joshua, to be weakened. He had just seen one of the greatest moves of God in the history of man—the opening of the Jordan River and the destruction of the city of Jericho—without the loss of a single Israelite. So, why would he now question the Lord?

If there is a problem, then it's not the Lord's fault, but rather ours.

### GET UP!

*"And the LORD said unto Joshua, Get thee up; wherefore liest thou thus upon thy face? Israel has sinned, and they have also transgressed my covenant which I commanded them: for they have even taken of the accursed thing, and have also stolen, and dissembled also, and they have put it even among their own stuff. Therefore the children of Israel could not stand before their enemies, but turned their backs before their enemies, because they were accursed: neither will I be*

*with you any more, except you destroy the accursed from among*
*you"* (Josh. 7:10-12).

The Lord said in verse 11, *"Israel hath sinned."* One sin
brought all of the nation to defeat and caused God to stop His
blessings. In fact, it was one sin that caused Adam and the whole
race to be under the present curse (Gen. 2:19; Rom. 5:12-21).
One sin brings the same result as committing all sins, at least
as far as sin itself is concerned (James 2:9-10).

It is certainly true that some sins are worse than others. Jesus
said so (John 19:11). But yet, as stated, even one sin makes a
person a sinner.

When Christians start bragging about the fact that they have
not committed certain sins, thinking this makes them better
than others, they need to think again.

There are thousands of individuals who are incarcerated in
penal institutions who did not kill anyone, but, still, they are
in prison just the same because of committing other types of
crime. As stated, some sins are definitely worse than others, but
all sin is grievously bad!

## SANCTIFY YOURSELVES

*Up, sanctify the people, and say, Sanctify yourselves against*
*to morrow: for thus says the LORD God of Israel, There is an*
*accursed thing in the midst of thee, O Israel: thou canst stand*
*before thine enemies, until ye take away the accursed thing from*
*among you. In the morning therefore ye shall be brought accord-*
*ing to your tribes: and it shall be, that the tribe which the LORD*

> *takes shall come according to the families thereof; and the family*
> *which the* LORD *shall take shall come by households; and the*
> *household which the* LORD *shall take shall come man by man.*
> *And it shall be, that he who is taken with the accursed thing*
> *shall be burnt with fire, he and all that he hath: because he*
> *hath transgressed the covenant of the* LORD, *and because he*
> *hath wrought folly in Israel* (Josh. 7:13-15).

Going back, Joshua 7:12 proclaims the greatest example that God will not bless anyone if there is unconfessed sin in one's life. As He wouldn't bless Israel because of Achan, likewise, He will not bless us presently if we harbor sin.

The *"accursed thing"* falls into many categories. The only way it can be defeated is for the believer to express his faith exclusively in Christ and what Christ has done for us at the cross. Then and only then can and will the Holy Spirit work within one's life. He alone can remove the accursed thing (Rom. 6:1-14; 8:1-11; I Cor. 1:17-18, 23; Gal. 6:14; Col. 2:10-15).

The enemies of the Lord would claim that the demand by the Lord that Achan and his family be killed is barbaric; however, the truth is, it is the sin that is barbaric because it allows Satan to steal, kill, and destroy (John 10:10). Instructions had been plainly and clearly given to the entirety of the army of Israel that no spoil was to be taken in Jericho by the soldiers or anyone else of the tribes of Israel. So to disobey this was to do so in the face of God with defiance and arrogance, which if allowed to continue, would wreck Israel.

If someone has a contagious disease, it is not cruel to quarantine that person where he cannot infect others. In fact, it would be cruel not to do so. No, the Lord was not cruel in what He demanded; He would have been cruel not to have done so.

## SIN AND THE CROSS

I do not personally believe that any Christian can properly understand sin until he first of all understands the cross. It was at the cross that all sin was addressed and properly atoned. To be sure, it was our sins that put Him there. Once one sees the cross properly, then one begins to see sin in its proper light. I'm referring to the cross as it applies to our everyday life and living. It's not a pretty picture. The reason that one can then see and understand sin to a greater degree is because one now properly sees oneself. Again, the picture is not pleasant to behold.

The cross of Christ shows everything for what it actually is. It tells us how black sin is and how ungodly we are. None of us enjoy very much hearing such a truth.

When one properly sees the cross—and I said properly—one then properly sees his own unrighteousness. He begins to see and understand that his only hope is in Christ and what Christ did at the cross. He ceases to look to his own righteousness and realizes how far short it falls. Once again, all of this comes about because of a proper understanding of the cross. Regrettably, not many in the modern church understand the cross, at least as it refers to our sanctification. Quite possibly, they don't desire to understand it, and for all the obvious reasons.

The cross of Christ exposes man for what he really is—totally unable to save himself in any capacity—and Christ for who He really is—the Savior of mankind, and the only Savior of mankind. Man is not too happy about admitting to either.

## WHY WERE ISRAEL'S SINS SO BAD AS IT REGARDED JERICHO?

All sin constitutes a breaking of the commandments of the Lord. In other words, we do what He tells us not to do.

Why is that so bad?

God knows where sin leads. He knows that it is the cause of all heartache, destruction, pain, sickness, suffering, and sorrow. He knows what the end result will be. It's like the spread of a contagious disease. If it's not stopped, it will destroy everything in its path. We only see the immediate results of sin, and that only in part. God sees sin and the bitter results even unto the bitter end.

Very near our office in Baton Rouge, Louisiana, they are building an interchange on Interstate 10. They recently placed some huge concrete crossbeams across the entirety of the highway where another crossway will be built. They found a crack in one of those giant crossbeams and demanded immediately that all work stop, at least as it regarded the crossbeams.

They were concerned that saltwater from Hurricane Katrina had gotten into the crack and onto the steel reinforcements. That could cause it to rust, thereby, weakening the crossbeam, which could cause a catastrophe in the future. Thankfully, the water had not reached the steel reinforcement and so there was no damage.

That is similar to sin. No matter how strong we may think we are, and that goes for every part of our life and living, sin will tear down the very strongest (even entire nations), as it has wrecked empires in the past. In fact, America's greatest danger is sin!

## WHY IS THE CROSS SO IMPORTANT?

The cross alone deals with sin. Nothing else will as nothing else can. This is the reason the cross of Christ is so important. Actually, it is the single most important thing that mankind faces. Without the cross, there is no remission of sin. When we use the term *the cross*, we are actually speaking of what Jesus did there in the giving of Himself in the shedding of His own precious blood (Eph. 2:13-18). That's the reason the church sins so greatly when it ignores the cross and, thereby, substitutes its own so-called remedy. It is the story of Cain all over again.

We've said it repeatedly, and we'll say it again: The only thing standing between mankind and eternal hell is the cross of Christ.

The only thing standing between the church and total apostasy is the cross of Christ.

Paul said:

> But this man (this Priest, Christ Jesus), *after He had offered one sacrifice for sins forever* (speaks of the cross), *sat down on the right hand of God* (refers to the great contrast with the priests under the Levitical system, who never sat down because their work was never completed; the work of Christ was a 'finished work' and needs no repetition);

*From henceforth expecting till His enemies be made His footstool.* (These enemies are Satan and all fallen angels and demon spirits, plus all who follow Satan.) *For by one offering He has perfected forever them who are sanctified.* (Everything one needs is found in the cross and the cross alone [Gal. 6:14]) (Heb. 10:12-14). – The Expositor's Study Bible

## OBEYING THE LORD

*"So Joshua rose up early in the morning, and brought Israel by their tribes; and the tribe of Judah was taken: And he brought the family of Judah; and he took the family of the Zarhites: and he brought the family of the Zarhites man by man; and Zabdi was taken: And he brought his household man by man; and Achan, the son of Carmi, the son of Zabdi, the son of Zerah, of the tribe of Judah, was taken"* (Josh. 7:16-18).

We find in all of this that sin is a terrible detriment to the forward motion of the work of God, whether in our immediate lives or whether in the work of the Lord in general.

It is the work of the Holy Spirit in our lives to rid us of all sin, exactly as He functioned in this scenario of our study.

While the Bible doesn't teach sinless perfection, it most definitely does teach victory over sin, and in every capacity. In other words, it teaches us that as believers, sin should not dominate us in any fashion. This can be accomplished only by the believer looking exclusively to Christ and the cross, which then gives the Holy Spirit latitude to work within our lives. He alone can bring about the desired results (Rom. 6:14).

## A LACK OF REPENTANCE?

There is no hint in the text that Achan sincerely repented. After the Holy Spirit had pointedly marked him as the guilty one, still, he only admitted what was done, and that was because he had no choice. There seemed to be no true contrition and no true repentance before God. While he possibly was sorry, it seems that he was only sorry that he was caught.

## SIN

> And Joshua said unto Achan, My son, give, I pray thee, glory to the LORD God of Israel, and make confession unto him; and tell me now what thou hast done; hide it not from me. And Achan answered Joshua, and said, Indeed I have sinned against the LORD God of Israel, and thus and thus have I done: When I saw among the spoils a goodly Babylonish garment, and two hundred shekels of silver, and a wedge of gold of fifty shekels weight, then I coveted them, and took them; and, behold, they are hid in the earth in the midst of my tent, and the silver under it.( Josh. 7:19-21 ).

Verse 21 says that Achan's sin was *"a goodly Babylonish garment, and two hundred shekels of silver, and a wedge of gold of fifty shekels weight."* Achan had heard the command, *"And ye, in any wise keep yourselves from the accursed thing"* ( Josh. 6:18).

It seems that Achan had no regard for the Word of God and was apparently accompanied by very little temptation. Babylon and money have a fateful attraction for the Christian. He found these things among the unconverted around him as they found them in Jericho, and his heart coveted them. This explains at least a part of the weakness of the modern church.

These sins are enjoyed instead of being confessed and forsaken. God has, therefore, withdrawn His power, and there is universal weakness and defeat. Fellowship with God can only be enjoyed if resolute separation from all evil be observed.

It seems that Achan's family joined with him in the stealing of these items and in their hiding of them. They would also join with him in the judgment. Furthermore, Joshua 7:5 says that their sin had caused the death of *"about thirty and six men"*. The wages of sin is (always) death. (Rom. 6:23).

## WILLFUL SIN AND UNWILLFUL SIN

There are two places in the Bible that pointedly declare willful sin, while it alludes to willful sin many other times.

Paul describes a willful sin:

*For if we sin wilfully* (the 'willful sin' is the transference of faith from Christ and Him crucified to other things) *after that we have received the knowledge of the truth* (speaks of the Bible way of salvation and victory, which is 'Jesus Christ and Him crucified' [I Cor. 2:2]), *there remains no more sacrifice for sins* (if the cross of Christ is rejected, there is no other sacrifice or way God will accept), *But a certain fearful looking for of judgment and fiery indignation* (refers to God's anger because of men rejecting Jesus Christ and the cross), *which shall devour the adversaries.* (It is hellfire, which will ultimately come to all who reject Christ and the cross.) *He who despised Moses' law died without mercy under two or three witnesses* (there had to be these many witnesses to a capital crime before the death sentence could be carried out, according to the Old Testament law of Moses [Deut. 17:2-7]): *Of how much sorer punishment, suppose ye, shall he be thought worthy, who has trodden under foot the Son of God* (proclaims the reason for the 'sorer punishment'), *and has counted the blood of the covenant, wherewith he was sanctified, an unholy thing* (refers to a person who has been saved but is now expressing unbelief toward that which originally saved him), *and has done despite unto the Spirit of grace?* (When the cross is rejected, the Holy Spirit is insulted.) *For we know Him who has said, Vengeance belongs unto Me, I will recompense, says the Lord* (is meant to imply that every single thing is going to be judged by the Lord, who alone is the righteous judge). *And again, The Lord shall judge His people* (chastise His people [Deut. 32:35-36]). *It is a fearful thing to fall into the hands of the living God.* (This refers to those who have once known the Lord but now express no faith in the cross) (Heb. 10:26-31) – The Expositor's Study Bible

## ENEMIES OF THE CROSS

Paul again dealt with the subject:

*Beware of dogs* (the apostle is addressing the Judaizers, who were Jews from Jerusalem who claimed Christ but insisted on believers keeping the law as well; all of this was diametrically opposed to Paul's gospel of the cross, in which the law of Moses had no part; as well, by the use of the word 'dogs,' the apostle was using the worst slur; in fact, the word 'dogs' was used by Jews for homosexuals; so, Paul is, in essence, saying that these Judaizers were to the gospel of Jesus Christ as homosexuality is to the human race—a perversion of the worst order), *beware of evil workers* (they denigrated the cross), *beware of the concision.* (This presents a Greek word Paul uses as a play upon the Greek word 'circumcision,' which was at the heart of the law gospel of the Judaizers) (Phil. 3:2).

The apostle then said:

*Brethren, be followers together of me* (be 'fellow-imitators'), *and mark them which walk so as you have us for an ensample* (observe intently). *For many walk* (speaks of those attempting to live for God outside of the victory and rudiments of the cross of Christ), *of whom I have told you often, and now tell you even weeping* (this is a most serious matter), *that they are the enemies of the cross of Christ* (those who do not look exclusively to the cross of Christ must be labeled 'enemies'): *Whose end is destruction* (if the cross is ignored, and continues to be ignored, the loss of the soul is the only ultimate conclusion), *whose god is their belly* (refers to those who attempt to pervert the gospel for their own personal gain), *and whose glory is in their shame* (the material things they seek, God labels as 'shame'), *who mind earthly things.* (This means they have no interest in heavenly things, which signifies they are using the Lord for their own personal gain. That is willful sin!) (Phil. 3:17-19) – The Expositor's Study Bible

## UNWILLFUL SIN

This sin concerns sin in which the believer engages but doesn't want to do so. In fact, he is trying with all of his might and strength not to do so, but he's trying in all the wrong ways, with the conclusion being that he fails anyway. Romans 7 is replete with this information. Please understand that even though its unwillful sin, it is still sin in the eyes of God, and the end result will be very hurtful unless the problem is properly addressed.

When Paul wrote Romans 7, he was writing about himself; however, the information given pertained to the time immediately after his conversion and baptism with the Holy Spirit, but yet, with a lack of knowledge as it regarded how to live for God. For a period of time, possibly even several years, he tried to live for God by the keeping of commandments. Regrettably and sadly, it was almost identical to the manner in which most of the modern church functions.

However, when he wrote Romans 7, he understood perfectly the ways of the Lord as it regarded victory because the Lord had recently given him the revelation as it regarded the meaning of the new covenant. More particularly, He had given Paul the sanctification part of the new covenant. That, in effect, was and is the meaning of the cross. Inspired by the Holy Spirit, the apostle told us that unless we follow the prescribed order laid down by the Lord (found in Romans 6, among other places), we will repeat Romans 7 all over again, no matter how hard we may try to function otherwise. In other words, the sin nature, which results in the *"law of sin and death,"* is ruling in such a believer's life.

## THE SIN NATURE

Let me say it again: Regrettably, due to modern believers having such little knowledge of the cross, the sin nature is ruling most Christians. I speak of Christians having little knowledge of the cross as it refers to sanctification—how we grow in grace and the knowledge of the Lord, and how we have victory over the world, the flesh, and the devil. Perhaps Romans 7 can be summed up in verse 15. The apostle said:

*For that which I do* (the failure) *I allow not* (should have been translated, 'I understand not'; these are not the words of an unsaved man, as some claim, but rather a believer who is trying and failing): *for what I would, that do I not* (refers to the obedience he wants to render to Christ, but rather fails; why? as Paul explained, the believer is married to Christ but is being unfaithful to Christ by spiritually cohabiting with the law, which frustrates the grace of God; that means the Holy Spirit will not help such a person, which guarantees failure [Gal. 2:21]); *but what I hate, that do I* (refers to sin in his life which he doesn't want to do and, in fact, hates, but finds himself unable to stop; unfortunately, due to the fact of not understanding the cross as it refers to sanctification, this is the plight of most modern Christians) (Rom. 7:15) – The Expositor's Study Bible

Now, don't misunderstand. As we've previously stated, even though such a believer (even as Paul) is trying not to fail the Lord and, in fact, hates the failure, still, sin will always bring forth very negative results. But yet, as should be obvious, God looks at such a person in a different light than He does those who are engaging in willful sin. Both Paul and Achan are perfect examples.

Achan engaged in willful sin while Paul engaged in unwillful sin, but let not the believer think that simply because it is unwillful, God overlooks the situation. The party is still guilty, and the end result is going to be extremely hurtful. In fact, even though it is unwillful sin in such a life, the situation will get worse and worse, with the sin becoming more and more pronounced.

## WILLPOWER

Unfortunately, most Christians are trying to live for God by the means of willpower, which cannot be done.

Some erroneously think that when they give their hearts to Christ, the Lord greatly strengthens their will in order for them to say no to sin, etc. That's not the way it is!

The Lord doesn't strengthen the willpower of anyone. While the will is definitely important—"Whosoever *will*"—still, within itself, it's not enough.

Listen again to Paul:

*For I know that in me (that is, in my flesh,) dwells no good thing* (speaks of man's own ability, or rather the lack thereof in comparison to the Holy Spirit, at least when it comes to spiritual things): *for to will is present with me* (Paul is speaking here of his willpower; regrettably, most modern Christians are trying to live for God by means of willpower, thinking falsely that since they have come to Christ, they are now free to say no to sin; that is the wrong way to look at the situation; the believer cannot live for God by the strength of willpower; while the will is definitely important, it alone is not enough; the believer must exercise faith in Christ and the cross, and do so constantly; then he will have the ability and strength to say yes to Christ, which automatically says no to the things of the world); *but how to perform that which is good I find not* (outside of the cross, it is impossible to find a way to do that which is scriptural) (Rom. 7:18). – The Expositor's Study Bible

## SPIRITUAL ADULTERY

Any individual who is trying to live for God by means other than faith in Christ and the cross, and faith in Christ and the cross exclusively, is living in a state of spiritual adultery. What does that mean?

Every believer is married to Christ (Rom. 7:1-4; II Cor. 11:1-4). In this state, Christ is to meet our every need and, in fact, is the only one who can meet our every need. However, when we begin to look to other than Christ and the cross, we are being unfaithful to Christ. That is spiritual adultery. Listen again to Paul:

> *For if he who comes preaching another Jesus* (a Jesus who is not of the cross), *whom we have not preached* (Paul's message was 'Jesus Christ and Him crucified'; anything else is 'another Jesus'), *or if you receive another spirit* (which is produced by preaching another Jesus), *which you have not received* (that's not what you received when we preached the true gospel to you), *or another gospel, which you have not accepted* (anything other than 'Jesus Christ and Him crucified' is 'another gospel'), *you might well bear with him.* (The apostle is telling the Corinthians they have, in fact, sinned because they tolerated these false apostles who had come in, bringing 'another gospel,' which was something other than Christ and the cross) (II Cor. 11:4). – The Expositor's Study Bible

Once again, that is spiritual adultery. That means that any believer who is making the object of his faith anything other than Christ and the cross is living in a state of spiritual adultery.

You can imagine how that hurts and hinders the Spirit of God within our lives. Thank God that in such situations, the Spirit does not leave us, but it does close the door to all the great things that He can do for us. As long as our faith is in anything other than Christ and the cross, we greatly tie the hands, so to speak, of the Spirit of God. Such guarantees failure on our part.

## THE FLESH

Any effort we make in trying to live for God outside of Christ and the cross is, in effect, the flesh. Now, what is the flesh?

It is that which is indicative to a human being, such as our personal talent, ability, education, motivation, knowledge, etc. In other words, it's what a human being can do. While those things are not necessarily sin within themselves, the facts are that we simply cannot live for God by the means of the flesh. Again listen to Paul:

> *That the righteousness of the law might be fulfilled in us* (the law finding its full accomplishment in us can only be done by faith in Christ and what Christ has done for us at the cross), *who walk not after the flesh* (not after our own strength and ability), *but after the Spirit* (the word 'walk' refers to the manner in which we order our lives; when we place our faith in Christ and the cross, understanding that all things come from God to us by means of the cross, ever making it the object of our faith, the Holy Spirit can then work mightily within us, bringing about the fruit of the Spirit; that is what 'walking after the Spirit' actually means!). *For they who are after the flesh do mind the things of the flesh* (refers to believers trying to live for the Lord by means other than faith in the cross of Christ); *but they who are after the Spirit the things of the Spirit* (those who place their faith in Christ and the cross, do so exclusively; they are doing what the Spirit desires, which alone can bring victory) (Rom. 8:4-5). – The Expositor's Study Bible

Paul continues: *"So then they that are in the flesh cannot please God* (refers to the believer attempting to live this Christian life by means other than faith in Christ and the cross)*"* (Rom. 8:8).

## WHY IS THE CROSS SO IMPORTANT?

Paul answered that question also:

*Blotting out the handwriting of ordinances that was against us* (pertains to the law of Moses, which was God's standard of righteousness that man could not reach), *which was contrary to us* (law is against us simply because we are unable to keep its precepts no matter how hard we try. While law shows the way, it provides no strength to walk in that way), *and took it out of the way* (refers to the penalty of the law being removed), *nailing it to His cross* (the law with its decrees was abolished in Christ's death as if crucified with Him); *And having spoiled principalities and powers* (Satan and all of his henchmen were defeated at the cross by Christ atoning for all sin; sin was the legal right Satan had to hold man in captivity; with all sin atoned, he has no more legal right to hold anyone in bondage), *He* (Christ) *made a show of them openly* (what Jesus did at the cross was in the face of the whole universe), *triumphing over them in it.* (The triumph is complete, and it was all done for us, meaning we can walk in power and perpetual victory due to the cross) (Col. 2:14-15).
– The Expositor's Study Bible

The moment we add any rule or regulation to the finished work of Christ, we have just abrogated the grace of God.

At the cross, the Lord satisfied the sin debt that every person owed but could not pay. As well, by atoning for all sin, this removed the legal right that Satan had to hold man captive. So, if man is captive now, it is because he does not function according to God's way, which is the cross of Christ. In fact, the cross opened the door for everything that God has for us. All we have to do to receive it is simply believe in Christ and what He did for us at the cross, and continue believing accordingly.

*Jesus keep me near the cross;*
*There a precious fountain,*
*Free to all, a healing stream,*
*Flows from Calvary's mountain.*

*Near the cross, a trembling soul,*
*Love and mercy found me;*
*There the bright and morning star*
*Shed its beams around me.*

*Near the cross, O Lamb of God,*
*Bring its scenes before me;*
*Help me walk from day to day*
*With its shadow o'er me.*

*Near the cross, I'll watch and wait,*
*Hoping, trusting ever,*
*Till I reach the golden strand,*
*Just beyond the river.*

# RAHAB

## AND OTHER

# MIRACLES

## VALLEY OF ACHOR

# VALLEY OF ACHOR

"SO JOSHUA SENT MESSENGERS, *and they ran unto the tent; and, behold, it was hid in his tent, and the silver under it. And they took them out of the midst of the tent, and brought them unto Joshua, and unto all the children of Israel, and laid them out before the* LORD. *And Joshua, and all Israel with him, took Achan the son of Zerah, and the silver, and the garment, and the wedge of gold, and his sons, and his daughters, and his oxen, and his asses, and his sheep, and his tent, and all that he had: and they brought them unto the valley of Achor. And Joshua said, Why hast thou troubled us? the* LORD *shall trouble thee this day. And all Israel stoned him with stones, and burned them with fire, after they had stoned them with stones. And they raised over him a great heap of stones unto this day. So the* LORD *turned from the fierceness of His anger. Wherefore the name of that place was called, the valley of Achor, unto this day*" ( Josh. 7:22-26).

Achan involved his family in the like ruin with himself. The use of the plural in the Hebrew text suggests that they, like Sapphira, were privy to the theft (Acts 5:1-2).

If the discovery and judgment of sin be painful, and if there be faithfulness in dealing with it, then grace gives both blessing and victory, and the valley of Achor becomes a door of hope (Hos. 2:15). In other words, if true repentance is engaged, the Lord will always forgive (I John 1:9).

## THE JUDGMENT OF GOD

As we've already stated, there is no evidence that Achan or any member of his family truly repented. As also stated, they were sorry they were caught, but as far as any true contrition before the Lord, none seems to be present; therefore, they had to suffer the just penalty of the law.

Why did the Lord forgive David of his terrible sin, which on the surface seemed to be much worse, and not forgive Achan and his family?

As Psalm 51 bears out, David truly repented, while, as stated, there is no evidence that Achan or his family repented at all. This is evident from the statement by Joshua when he said, *"Why hast thou troubled us? the LORD shall trouble thee this day."*

And yet, in the last verse of this chapter, we are given a note of hope with the words *"the valley of Achor."*

The prophet Hosea said, *"And I will give her her vineyards from thence, and the valley of Achor for a door of hope: and she shall sing there, as in the days of her youth, and as in the day when she came up out of the land of Egypt"* (Hos. 2:15).

*"The valley of Achor for a door of hope"* signals back to a vale of horror as described in Joshua 7:24, but it is to become a door

of hope for Israel and, as well, for all individuals, at least those who will subscribe to the grace of God. The truth is presented here by the Holy Spirit that where the wrath of God justly fell, the grace of God was to brightly shine. The valley of horror became the vale of hope. Such was Calvary—a place of horror to the suffering Savior under the wrath of God, but a door of hope to the redeemed sinner under the grace of God.

Thus, this valley of Achor proclaims to the believer who has suffered defeat that the area of such defeat can become his area of victory.

## FEAR NOT

*And the LORD said unto Joshua, Fear not, neither be thou dismayed: take all the people of war with thee, and arise, go up to Ai: see, I have given into thy hand the king of Ai, and his people, and his city, and his land: And thou shall do to Ai and her king as you did unto Jericho and her king: only the spoil thereof, and the cattle thereof, shall ye take for a prey unto yourselves: lay thee an ambush for the city behind it. So Joshua arose, and all the people of war, to go up against Ai: and Joshua chose out thirty thousand mighty men of valour, and sent them away by night. And he commanded them, saying, Behold, ye shall lie in wait against the city, even behind the city: go not very far from the city, but be ye all ready (Josh. 8:1-4).*

Victories are easily won in the path of simplicity and faith, but if sin has been indulged, it causes considerable pain to win even small victories. Even though sin had by now been put away, still, much difficulty was engaged in order to win the victory at Ai. All the people had to be mustered, and an ambushment had to be set—Israel had to pretend to flee! Nothing of this was seen in the capture of Jericho. So, the daring example is set before us!

## THE LORD WILL DELIVER

> *And I, and all the people who are with me, will approach unto the city: and it shall come to pass, when they come out against us, as at the first, that we will flee before them, (For they will come out after us) till we have drawn them from the city; for they will say, They flee before us, as at the first: therefore we will flee before them. Then ye shall rise up from the ambush, and seize upon the city: for the LORD your God will deliver it into your hand. And it shall be, when ye have taken the city, that ye shall set the city on fire: according to the commandment of the LORD shall ye do. See, I have commanded you* (Josh. 8:5-8).

The taking of these cities and the destruction of them, along with the need of the particular time, was, as well, symbolic of the victory that is to be won within our present-day lives and living. The promised land was God's land; consequently, all enemies had to be put to the sword. Likewise, we as believers now belong to the Lord. Everything in our lives that is not proper must be subjected to the sword of the Spirit, with the fire of the Spirit burning out the dross (Matt. 3:11; Eph. 6:17).

## A PERSONAL EXPERIENCE

On one of our trips to Israel, I asked the guide if he could take us to where the city of Ai had been located. As well, I wanted to follow the route that Joshua would have taken from Jericho to this particular place.

From Jericho to Ai, one has to cross a mountain range, and even though it's not far, still, the mountains have to be traversed. So, about the only way Joshua could have gone with his army was the way that we went because of the lay of the land. The guide related to us that there was no way that anyone presently could know where Ai did actually exist because no ruins remained. And yet, we were taken to the place that seemed to be the only logical site for the city where, no doubt, it had been situated.

Going up the mountain about halfway to the supposed site of Ai, one could look out over the entirety of the Jordan Valley, at least at that particular location. It is easy to see where Gilgal would have been located and where the Jordan was crossed, which was the opposite of Jericho.

## WHY WAS ALL OF THIS IMPORTANT TO ME?

I wanted to go to the site of Ai and go the way that Joshua, no doubt, went because it's in the Bible, and there is nothing more important than the Word of God.

In fact, that's what makes the entirety of the Holy land so very, very interesting. Were we speaking of mere historical narratives, that would be something else; however, inasmuch as we're speaking of the very site where these biblical events took place, in other words, where God was tremendously involved, then they become very important. At least they do to me.

When Joshua first went against Ai, there is no biblical record that he sought the Lord as to what he should do; consequently, defeat was his, with some thirty-six men dying. Now, he most definitely sought the Lord, and the Lord gave him explicit directions as it regarded how the city was to be approached. Had he prayed the first time, no doubt, the defeat could have been avoided.

We make a great mistake when we take the way of the Lord for granted. To be over confident is just as bad as to be faithless. Either way, self is in the way.

This means that the believer should seek the Lord about everything, even the things that seem to be small, which Ai at the beginning definitely seemed to be. However, small situations can turn into big situations, and fast, especially if we do not have the mind of the Lord.

## JOSHUA

*Joshua therefore sent them forth: and they went to lie in ambush, and abode between Bethel and Ai, on the west side of Ai: but Joshua lodged that night among the people. And Joshua rose up early in the morning, and numbered the people, and went up, he and the elders of Israel, before the people to Ai. And all the people, even the people of war who were with him, went up, and drew near, and came before the city, and pitched on the north side of Ai: now there was a valley between them and Ai. And he took about five thousand men, and set them to lie in ambush between Bethel and Ai, on the west side of the city. And when they had set the people, even all the host that was on the north of the city, and their liers in wait on the west of the city, Joshua went that night into the midst of the valley* (Josh. 8:9-13).

God numbered exactly those who would do battle in His service. It was then physical as well as spiritual; it is now altogether spiritual.

The fight at present is *"the good fight of faith"* (I Tim. 6:12). This fight in which we are called upon to engage pertains to our faith. This refers to one exclusively placing one's faith in Christ and the cross. The cross must never be separated from Christ, and we speak of its benefits (Eph. 2:13-18; Gal. 6:14).

## THE STRETCHED OUT SPEAR

*And it came to pass, when the king of Ai saw it, that they hasted and rose up early, and the men of the city went out against Israel to battle, he and all his people, at a time appointed, before the plain; but he wist not that there were liers in ambush against him behind the city. And Joshua and all Israel made as if they were beaten before them, and fled by the way of the wilderness. And all the people who were in Ai were called together to pursue after them: and they pursued after Joshua, and were drawn away from the city. And there was not a man left in Ai or Bethel, who went not out after Israel: and they left the city open, and pursued after Israel. And the LORD said unto Joshua, Stretch out the spear that is in thy hand toward Ai; for I will give it into thine hand. And Joshua stretched out the spear that he had in his hand toward the city* (Josh. 8:14-18).

The stretching out of the spear toward the city was a symbol of faith. God's plan is ever onward. He never retreats, never goes backward, and never loses ground. As stated, it is always forward.

God honors faith, and God honors only faith. However, we must ever understand that the faith that God honors is that which has as its object the cross of Christ. This is overly important. Just to have faith doesn't say much. In fact, every human being in the world, meaning all unsaved people, has faith. It's faith in themselves or faith in one thing or the other, but it is definitely not faith in Christ and what He did for us at the cross.

As it regards believers, most fall into the same category. Most of the faith of believers is the same type of faith that's in the world (faith in themselves), or if they are trying to be more spiritual, they'll say that it's faith in the Word, etc. That should be the case, but that which says too much in actuality says very little.

The story of the Bible from cover to cover is *"Jesus Christ, and him crucified"* (I Cor. 1:17; 2:2). Faith in Christ and what Christ has done for us at the cross is the only thing that God will recognize. We must never forget that. This is the secret of all victory.

## THEY TOOK THE CITY

*And the ambush arose quickly out of their place, and they ran as soon as he had stretched out his hand: and they entered into the city, and took it, and hasted and set the city on fire. And when the men of Ai looked behind them, they saw, and, behold, the smoke of the city ascended up to heaven, and they had no power to flee this way or that way: and the people that fled to the wilderness turned back upon the pursuers. And when Joshua and all Israel saw that the ambush had taken the city, and that the smoke of the city ascended, then they turned again, and slew the men of Ai. And the other issued out of the city against them; so they were in the midst of Israel, some on this side, and some on that side: and they smote them, so that they let none of them remain or escape. And the king of Ai they took alive, and brought him to Joshua (Josh. 8:19-23).*

Everything in our lives that is not proper with the Lord must be slain and can be slain, but it is only by the believer placing his faith in Christ and the cross (Rom. 6:3-14).

## VICTORY OVER THE ENEMY

The Lord gave Joshua minute instructions as to how he was to proceed regarding the taking of the city of Ai. Joshua was not to deviate one iota from those instructions. As is obvious, it was the word of the Lord, and the account is given to us in the Bible.

It is the same presently. We must not deviate from the Word of the Lord in any respect. If we stay true to the Word, victory in every capacity will be ours. If we forsake the Word for our own meanderings, there will be no victory. Regrettably and sadly, that's exactly what the modern church is doing. It is functioning in the strength of its own mental stratagems, with the Word of God given little consideration, if any at all. As a result, while there is much machinery and much activity, the truth is, precious few are getting saved, precious few are being delivered, and precious few are being baptized with the Holy Spirit.

## THE CROSS OF CHRIST IS THE FOUNDATION OF ALL VICTORY

Many Christians have it in their minds that if they are not bound by alcohol, drugs, nicotine, immorality, etc., then everything is well and good. The truth is, there are millions of people who do not know the Lord and make no claim on the Lord whatsoever, who are not bound by those things either. In fact, those things are but symptoms of the real problem, with the real problem being self. Now we're getting down, proverbially speaking, to where the rubber meets the road.

Most Christians have had so little instruction as it regards self that they have very little idea of what one is talking about when this subject is broached. However, Paul had more to say about self, which he referred to as the flesh, than anything else. The Holy Spirit did this because this is the real problem with the child of God. There is no way that self can be put in its proper place without the believer understanding the cross, which alone is the answer for self and sin. So, if the believer ignores the cross, disbelieves the message of the cross, or is ignorant as it regards the cross, there will be precious little victory regarding self as it pertains to such believers. The truth is that the Holy Spirit alone can perfect our lives as they should be. Even then, it is definitely not easy, and neither is it done quickly. In fact, Job is the great example of such in the Word of God.

## DESTROYED ALL

*And it came to pass, when Israel had made an end of slaying all the inhabitants of Ai in the field, in the wilderness wherein they chased them, and when they were all fallen on the edge of the sword, until they were consumed, that all the Israelites returned unto Ai, and smote it with the edge of the sword. And so it was, that all who fell that day, both of men and women, were twelve thousand, even all the men of Ai. For Joshua drew not his hand back, wherewith he stretched out the spear, until he had utterly destroyed all the inhabitants of Ai* (Josh. 8:24-26).

The individuals of Ai were so steeped in sin and idolatry that one archeologist stated, "The God of Israel, who gave instructions that all of these heathen tribes in the land of Canaan be exterminated, did future generations an untold service."

Another archeologist stated, "The evil in which these people engaged themselves, such as incest, bestiality, homosexuality, as well as wholesale human sacrifice to idols, so corrupted them that their destruction to protect other nations and future generations was demanded.

## MAJOR SURGERY

> *Only the cattle and the spoil of that city Israel took for a prey unto themselves, according unto the word of the LORD which He commanded Joshua. And Joshua burnt Ai, and made it an heap forever, even a desolation unto this day. And the king of Ai he hanged on a tree until eventide: and as soon as the sun was down, Joshua commanded that they should take his carcase down from the tree, and cast it at the entering of the gate of the city, and raise thereon a great heap of stones, that remaineth unto this day* (Josh. 8:27-29).

The moral of all of this is: if weights and sins in our lives aren't exterminated, which can only be exterminated by the cross, they will ultimately wreck us (Heb. 12:1-2).

Extermination of these idolaters was demanded by the Lord because to do otherwise would have put Israel in great danger. It is the same with sin in our present-day lives. It must be exterminated, which means to be rooted out completely, or else, it will ultimately exterminate us. One or the other must go!

## THE HOLY SPIRIT AND THE CROSS OF CHRIST

Before the cross, where the sin debt was forever settled, animal blood served as a stopgap measure, so to speak, but was woefully inadequate. In fact, animal blood in the realm of clean animals, such as lambs, etc., could not remove the terrible sin debt; therefore, it remained unpaid.

Because of such, the Holy Spirit could not come into hearts and lives to abide permanently. In fact, He could only come into the hearts of a certain few, actually, those who had been called for a specific task. He helped them to perform that task (I Sam. 16:13) and then departed. That's why Jesus said to His disciples the week of His passion, *"Even the Spirit of truth; whom the world cannot receive, because it seeth him not, neither knoweth him: but ye know him; for he dwelleth with you, and shall be in you.* (John 14:17).

Plainly and simply, our Lord told His disciples and all other believers that while the Holy Spirit most definitely dwelt with them, He did not at that time (before the cross) dwell in them. This would come about after the cross.

## AFTER THE CROSS

After the cross, Jesus atoned for all sin—past, present, and future—at least for all who will believe (John 3:16; Col. 2:14-15). This paid the sin debt, and paid it totally and completely, with nothing left over. As a result, the Holy Spirit can come into the heart and life of the believer and dwell there permanently, which He most definitely does at conversion (I Cor. 3:16). It's all due to the cross. In other words, it's the cross that made it possible for the Holy Spirit to make the believer His permanent home.

As a result, the Holy Spirit works entirely within the framework of the finished work of Christ. In fact, He will work no other way.

Paul said, *"For the law of the Spirit of life in Christ Jesus hath made me free from the law of sin and death"* (Rom. 8:2).

We are told in this verse that this is a law, meaning that it is a law that was devised by the Godhead sometime in eternity past.

The phrase, *"in Christ Jesus,"* always and without exception refers to what Christ did at the cross. So this law of the way the Spirit works is ensconced totally and completely in Christ Jesus, referring to what He did for us at the cross. That's the reason that we boldly proclaim that the Holy Spirit will not work outside of the framework of the cross of Christ. The cross is what gives Him the legal right to do what He does in our lives, hence, the word *law* being used in this respect.

The Lord doesn't require much of us in this great plan, but He does require one thing, and that is faith. However, it must be faith in Christ and the cross, and Christ and the cross exclusively, or the Holy Spirit is greatly hindered, thereby, unable to develop His fruit within our lives.

## THE CROSS AND PERFECTION

As previously stated, the Bible does not teach sinless perfection as it regards the child of God. In fact, that will not come about until the first resurrection of life when we shall be changed (I Cor. 15). And yet, it does teach perfection, but it is perfection that is in Christ, and Christ alone.

When the believer places his faith exclusively in Christ and what Christ has done for us at the cross, our Lord then gives us His perfection, which is all done by grace (the goodness of God).

The whole burnt offering of the Old Testament proclaims Christ giving the believer His perfection (His all)! The sin offering presents Christ taking on Himself all of our sin. So, we have the former offering giving us His perfection, while the latter offering takes all of our sin.

In fact, these particular offerings of the Old Testament were types and shadows, while the cross of Christ is the fulfillment of such. Righteousness is imputed to the believer only as the believer exercises faith in Christ and the cross. If the believer tries to bring about righteousness by his own machinations, the only thing that he will develop is self-righteousness. Even though saved and baptized with the Holy Spirit, still, within ourselves, we cannot perfect anything in our hearts and lives that needs to be perfected. That can be done only by the Holy Spirit.

Let us say it again: Our faith must be anchored squarely in Christ and the cross, and remain squarely in Christ and the cross, even renewing it on a daily basis (Luke 9:23). With this being done, continuing to be done, and, in fact, never ceasing to be done, the Holy Spirit can then work mightily, thereby, developing His fruit, which translates into righteousness and holiness (Rom. 6, 8; Gal. 5).

## THE ALTAR

*"Then Joshua built an altar unto the LORD God of Israel in Mount Ebal, As Moses the servant of the LORD commanded the children of Israel, as it is written in the book of the law of Moses, an altar*

*of whole stones, over which no man hath lift up any iron; and they offered thereon burnt offerings unto the LORD, and sacrificed peace offerings. And he wrote there upon the stones a copy of the law of Moses, which he wrote in the presence of the children of Israel"* (Josh. 8:30-32).

According to the Word of the Lord, the altar was built on Mount Ebal, the mount of cursing, which relates to the curse of sin, and not Mount Gerizim, the mount of blessing.

Christ alone perfectly obeyed the law; therefore, as a man, He enjoyed its blessing. Yet, in love for those who had incurred its curse because of their sinning, He voluntarily ascended the hill of malediction, and in His own person, He suffered the judgment. Thus, He brought out from under the curse those who were sentenced to death (Gal. 3:13-14).

Regrettably, the modern church is attempting to build the altar, i.e., the cross, that is, if the cross is considered at all, on Mount Gerizim, the mount of blessing. This is a denial of the real problem of man, which is sin.

The altar—a type of the cross—was built of stones and unshaped. It symbolized the fact that we must not add to the cross or take from the cross.

## ALL THAT IS WRITTEN IN THE BOOK

*And all Israel, and their elders, and officers, and their judges, stood on this side the ark and on that side before the priests the Levites, which bare the ark of the covenant of the LORD, as well the stranger, as he who was born among them; half of them over against Mount Gerizim, and half of them over against Mount Ebal; as Moses the servant of the Lord had commanded before, that they should bless the people of Israel. And afterward he read all the words of the law, the blessings and cursings, according to all that is written in the book of the law. There was not a word of all that Moses commanded, which Joshua read not before all the congregation of Israel, with the women, and the little ones, and the strangers who were conversant among them* (Josh. 8:33-35).

All of Israel stood at the foot of Mount Gerizim, the mount of blessing, where the ark of the covenant was then located, and pronounced blessings upon Israel. However, let it be understood that all of these blessings were predicated on a proper understanding of the altar and its use.

It is incumbent upon us presently as preachers of the gospel to announce to the entirety of the church the Word of the Lord, taking nothing from it and adding nothing to it.

Unfortunately, we presently have churches that we might refer to as "blessing churches," which means that blessing is all they pronounce. Then we have some that are all "cursing churches," meaning that they are constantly condemning the people. Both are wrong.

For the church to be what it ought to be, it must recognize that man's problem is sin, and the only solution to that problem is the cross of Christ. With that properly addressed, the blessing will automatically come. Unfortunately, there are very few modern churches that fall into the category of treating the problem as it should be treated. In fact, most do not even admit that the problem of the believer is sin. As previously stated many times, the only solution for sin is the cross of Christ. There is no other as there need be no other.

Men do not mind crosses, or altars one might say, of their own making. In fact, the church is full of them. However, it is the cross alone that the Bible pronounces that God will accept. He will accept nothing else. The story of Cain and Abel is a perfect type in point.

Cain did not deny that there was a God, and neither did he deny that He deserved an offering. He just didn't want to offer something that was not of his own doing. So, he refused the offering that God demanded, which was the slain lamb with its shed blood. This typified that man is a sinner and that there is no forgiveness of sin without the shedding of innocent blood, which speaks of Christ.

So, Cain offered up something of his own making. Abel offered up that which God demanded, and it was, thereby, accepted.

Please understand the following: God did not look at the ones bringing the offering, for it was obvious as to what they were. Both had been born outside of Eden, which means they were born as a product of the fall of their father Adam. Consequently, both were lost. So, God didn't even look at them. He rather looked at the offering. If the offering was right, the one bringing the offering was accepted. If the offering was rejected, then the one bringing that offering was rejected as well. It hasn't changed from then until now.

## THE WORD OF GOD

As well, linked with the altar was the Word of God. Verse 32 says, *"And he wrote there upon the stones a copy of the law of Moses, which he wrote in the presence of the children of Israel."* This Word of God was then read to all of Israel, including the little children and even the strangers who were among them.

This tells us that the Word of God is applicable to all. In fact, there is no such thing as a Western gospel or an Eastern gospel. There is only one gospel for the entirety of the world (John 3:16).

*When we walk with the Lord,*
*In the light of His Word,*
*What a glory He sheds on our way;*
*While we do His good will,*
*He abides with us still,*
*And with all who will trust and obey.*

*Not a shadow can rise,*
*Not a cloud in the skies,*
*But His smile quickly drives it away;*
*Not a doubt or a fear,*
*Not a sigh or a tear,*
*Can abide while we trust and obey.*

*Not a burden we bear,*
*Not a sorrow we share,*
*But our toil He does richly repay;*
*Not a grief or a loss,*
*Not a frown or a cross,*
*But is blest if we trust and obey.*

*But we never can prove*
*The delights of His love,*
*Until all on the altar we lay;*
*For the favour He shows,*
*And the joy He bestows,*
*Are for them who will trust and obey.*

*Then in fellowship sweet,*
*We will sit at His feet,*
*Or we'll walk by His side in the way;*
*What He says we will do;*
*Where He sends we will go,*
*Never fear, only trust and obey.*

# REFERENCES

## CHAPTER 1

[1] George Williams, *William's Complete Bible Commentary*, Grand Rapids, Kregel Publications, 1994 , Pg. 108.

## CHAPTER 2

[1] George Williams, *William's Complete Bible Commentary*, Grand Rapids, Kregel Publications, 1994 , Pg. 109.

[2] Ibid.

[3] Ibid.

[4] H.D.M. Spence, *The Pulpit Commentary: Joshua 2:12-24*, Grand Rapids, Eerdmans Publishing Company, 1978.

## CHAPTER 4

[1] George Williams, *William's Complete Bible Commentary*, Grand Rapids, Kregel Publications, 1994 , Pg. 110.

[2] Ibid, 111.

## CHAPTER 5

[1] George Williams, *William's Complete Bible Commentary*, Grand Rapids, Kregel Publications, 1994 , Pg. 111.

[2] Ibid, 112.

## CHAPTER 6

[1] George Williams, *William's Complete Bible Commentary*, Grand Rapids, Kregel Publications, 1994 , Pg. 25.

# ABOUT EVANGELIST JIMMY SWAGGART

The Rev. Jimmy Swaggart is a Pentecostal evangelist whose anointed preaching and teaching has drawn multitudes to the cross of Christ since 1955.

As an author, he has written more than 60 books, commentaries, study guides, and The Expositor's Study Bible, which has sold more than 4.5 million copies.

As an award-winning musician and singer, Brother Swaggart has recorded more than 60 gospel albums and sold nearly 17 million recordings worldwide.

For more than six decades, Brother Swaggart has channeled his preaching and music ministry through multiple media venues including print, radio, television and the Internet.

In 2010, Jimmy Swaggart Ministries launched its own cable channel, SonLife Broadcasting Network, which airs 24 hours a day to a potential viewing audience of more than 2 billion people around the globe.

Brother Swaggart also pastors Family Worship Center in Baton Rouge, Louisiana, the church home and headquarters of Jimmy Swaggart Ministries.

Jimmy Swaggart Ministries materials can be found at **www.jsm.org**.